To Edwin and Mary Ann, my grandparents.
To my parents, Edwin and Mary.
Also to Miss Gunning, a wonderful teacher
who made me feel very special, and who I have
always remembered with much affection.

Also in loving memory of our beautiful
daughter Virginia who was tragically taken
from us in the place she called 'Paradise'.
We will love and miss her always.

Virginia, 1962–2010

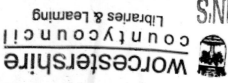
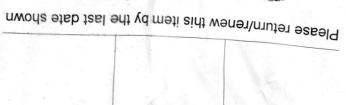

A Field
Full of
Butterflies

Memories of a
Romany Childhood

ROSEMARY PENFOLD

An Orion Paperback

First published in Great Britain in 2011
by Orion Books
an imprint of the Orion Publishing Group Ltd
Orion House, 5 Upper St Martin's Lane,
London, WC2H 9EA

An Hachette UK company

10 9 8 7 6 5

A CIP catalogue record for this book
is available from the British Library.

ISBN 978 1 4091 2095 7

Typeset at The Spartan Press Ltd,
Lymington, Hants

Printed and bound in Great Britain by
Clays Ltd, St Ives plc

The Orion Publishing Group's policy is to use papers that
are natural, renewable and recyclable products and made
from wood grown in sustainable forests. The logging and
manufacturing processes are expected to conform to the
environmental regulations of the country of origin.

www.orionbooks.co.uk

Preface

These are my memories and mine alone. If anyone says they remember it differently, I shall say, 'Well, those are your memories and yours alone.'

This book is written as a tribute to those of my family who have gone before, all worthy of remembrance, and to help non-Gypsies understand a little of how real Romanies lived in the early part of the twentieth century, not in misery or deprivation but enjoying a way of life that many today would envy and yearn for, even as I do still.

Rosemary Penfold

True Romanies or Gypsies are generally not understood by those who are not. Anyone who is different from the accepted 'norm', for whatever reason, can expect to be castigated by society in general. This happens from our childhood up, unless a decent education explains otherwise. This book does not set out to explore the political correctness of our modern day as regards Gypsies, or indeed any other minority group. Nor does it seek to find answers as to why man's inhumanity to man is often based on what we compare ourselves to, and which category we pigeonhole ourselves into. It delves into the life of one family who just happened to live on the cusp of a time when humankind's belief in a technological revolution brought an end to one way of life and gave birth to another. A time past, when a group of families could travel in complete freedom from one end of the country to another, in their own time with their own mode of transport and accommodation, partaking of water from village wells along the way and camping on common ground known as the village green. All that has changed, as it has in many parts of the world. Where are the Native Americans now? Is it a good thing that we all live identical lives in the huge melting pot of life, in identical boxes within identical streets? After all, we do not live in a 'one hat fits all' society. We do not judge all the people in one street to have the same values, morals and opinions as ourselves, just because of their chosen geographical location – or do we?

We are told that tolerance is the key to living in harmony with one another. Prejudice is the opposite. It is not pretending that there are no differences between us that make us equal; it is accepting and celebrating that there are.

Sarah Churchill

Thanks

Thanks to everyone at Orion Publishing (especially Celia, who worked so hard on my behalf), and to everyone at *The Alan Titchmarsh Show* for giving me the wonderful opportunity to have my book published – it's like a dream come true!

A big thank you to my daughter Sarah – I really could not have done it without you and your belief in me. Also to my husband John for his endless support and interest in every page, and his delight when he knew my book was to be published.

Thanks to my other children, Daniel and Claire, for your encouragement and belief in me, and for showing how proud you are of me. Your support means everything to me.

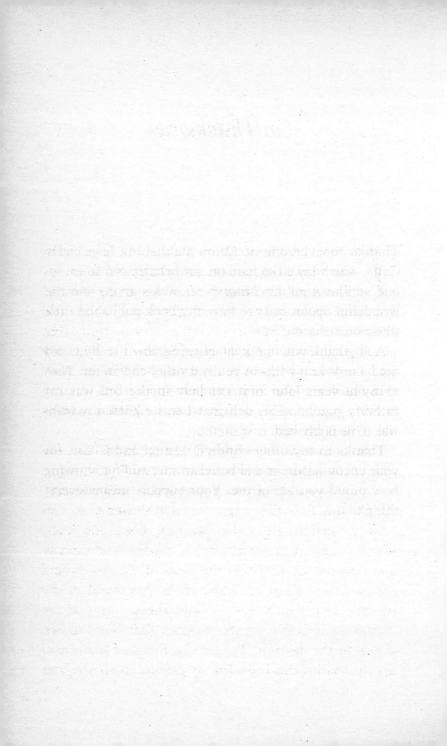

Early Memories

I sat on a hard floor. Above me soared a huge bed in which lay a tiny person, propped up on enormous billowy pillows. Two other people stood near the bed. They spoke quietly to each other and to the little person in the bed. I was chewing on something that tasted good. Someone kept bending down to wipe my face. I now know this to be my mother and father. They told me years later that the lady in the bed was my father's grandmother, and that I was eighteen months old. This is my very first memory.

I was born on St Valentine's Day, 1938 to one Romany parent (my father) and one *gadje* in a real Gypsy wagon or *vardoe* (a real Gypsy would never call it a caravan), the eldest of four. Our wagon stood in a camp of several homes consisting of other wagons, tents and huts, which belonged to aunts, uncles, cousins and Granny and Granfer. Granfer was the head of the family and presided over all of us. I arrived in this world in my parents' bed, which was set into the far wall of the wagon with heavy mirrored doors that were drawn across in the daytime. I spent the first few months of my life sharing this bed with my parents, as also in later years did my three brothers. By some miracle we all survived being squashed or suffocated. As I grew older, I was relegated to the lower bed, directly beneath my parents, also with doors that drew across. When I was eight, my father bought another wagon so I could have a bed to myself, as until then I had shared with my three younger siblings. This made the bed seem smaller, and it was uncomfortable, noisy and quarrelsome to say the least. I well remember staying awake for what seemed like hours, waiting for the latest addition to the family to stop screaming so that I could say my prayers, convinced that God would never be able to hear me above his cries.

I also experienced several very bad nights in this bed due to my eavesdropping, as one of my aunts recounted in hushed tones a story she had heard about a baby being born with two heads. I lay night after night, stiff with terror, convinced that this horror was crouched at the bottom of my bed, just waiting for me to fall asleep. I was always surprised to find myself alive and unscathed in the mornings.

The wagon was tiny inside, apart from the beds, but contained ingenious storage space for everything we could possibly need. There was a food cupboard, a little stove, a chair and a long cupboard on the left of the stove near the door in which our clothes were kept. Two large, blackened kettles were always on the stove, as was the heavy old smoothing iron, which our mother heated on the stove to iron our clothes. A brass toasting fork hung on a hook nearby. To the other side of the doorway was a long corner cupboard with a mirror above and a shelf below, on which a small aluminium bowl with a lump of carbolic was kept and an enamel jug for hand-washing. In the cupboard were my father's shaving accoutrements, including his cut-throat razor, strop, shaving brush, soap and hairbrush. Next to this were a bench seat and a small table under the window where my mother kept the teapot and made the tea. The willow-pattern china was kept above between the bed and the window in another corner cupboard that had glass doors with half-curtains made of pretty lace. The floor was covered with linoleum, the area being no more than about four feet by four feet. Yet six people managed to live in this tiny space. It must have seemed impossible to outsiders, with their big houses and other modern conveniences, but we managed very well, mainly because we were never indoors. From dawn until dusk, rain or shine, we played outside.

I can never remember having a cold or coughs, only the usual childhood ailments such as chicken pox and mumps. I well remember those times, as it was the only time I had my parents' undivided attention, and was even spoiled a little, which was a luxury. Once, when I had mumps, I was feeling really poorly and I remember the doctor whispering to my mother that I needed some vitamin C. My father disappeared and was gone all day. Late that night he came in with a large brown bag, which he emptied over the table. Oranges, lemons and a jar of honey rolled out and my mother made me lemon drinks to soothe my throat. Now I wonder how he was able to get them, as it was the war years and fruit was very difficult to get hold of. But my father always seemed to come up trumps.

Our lives were lived out in the fresh air. We cooked and ate outside, did the washing, shelled peas and a million other jobs besides. Later on, when I went to school one of my teachers once asked me, one bitterly cold winter, if we were cold in the caravan. I gazed at her in amazement.

'No, of course not,' I replied. 'We are lovely and warm!'

I could see she didn't believe me, poor soul, as she stared at me in pity. How could she possibly know how cosy and warm we were as we ate our huge plates of rabbit stew with doorsteps of bread and butter, the little stove glowing red hot and three candles sending dancing shadows up the wall?

Sunday night was bath night. My mother heated up the water in the clothes boiler and pulled out the old tin bath. The boiler was housed in a corrugated-tin roofed building with open sides and front as a doorway, that my father had built in the yard where our wagon was sited. We called this the 'wash house'. Wood was pushed into the burner below and water poured in at the top. This boiler was shared by all the families in the camp. In the summer we bathed outside, but when it was cold it was squeezed in front of the range in the wagon. We used the same water for all four of us. I always went first, wallowing in the luxury of warm, clean water which was topped up at intervals from a tall enamel jug. I have no doubt that it was pretty mucky after we had all used it. Then, not a drop was wasted, as it was put on the garden. This was followed by fresh clean underwear and then bed. In those days, this underwear had to last the whole week. Unthinkable now, but then we had very few clothes and washing was only done once a week. This was quite common among all children then.

Every Friday night without fail, Granny used to line us up and go through our hair with a nit comb. As my cousin Violet's and mine was waist length and worn in plaits, this was half an hour of torture. We didn't dare move, or she would thump our heads with the comb. She continued to drag the comb through our hair until she was satisfied that nothing was in it that shouldn't have been. It was a painful experience, but it must have worked because we never once caught head lice.

Monday was washday, whatever the weather. My father used to light the boiler at about seven in the morning so that it would be hot by about eight o'clock. My mother washed the sheets first as they had to be dried by the evening. One sheet per bed was all we had. These would be poked and prodded with a bleached wooden stick for the purpose, sending up clouds of steam that would envelop my mother. These would be rinsed by hand in cold water in the bathtub and then fed through the mangle, before being hung on the long line which ran all the way up the garden. Then in would go the coloureds, followed by the darks. This took the whole day, and by the time she had finished, my mother's hands were red raw and bleeding. If the sheets weren't quite dry by the afternoon, Mum would iron them with the heavy flat iron kept hot on the range. She would pull the table out to iron on, and wrap a cloth around the iron handle to save her hands from being burned. I always liked the bit when she would spit on the iron to see if it was hot enough.

I know very little about how my parents met. Mum would probably have told me had I asked, but my life was of the moment. Although I soaked up everything I saw and heard around me, I was not at all curious about the lives they had led before I was born. It was almost as though nothing had existed before I had. Mum told me she had been training to be a nurse and was already living in the town when they married. Dad probably met her when he knocked at my maternal grandmother, Granny-in-Town's, door, asking for any scrap they might want to sell. My father was a very handsome man when he was young, and resembled a young Cary Grant. I saw a photograph of him once at Granny's place. However it happened, they fell in love and married. My father thought my mother was very clever and admired her greatly, often praising her in front of others. Dad was strong and noisy, whereas Mum was quiet and gentle. She could lose her temper on rare occasions, but only for a very good reason.

She could be very stubborn when she needed to be, and often got her way by just going very quiet. My father found this too much to bear, and gave way to her although he obviously did not want to. To give her credit, she did not use this ploy very often. She knew Dad well enough to know that he would just get angry and we would all feel the brunt of his tongue. As it was, she knew when to stop.

When my mother married my father, she was

expected to integrate with his family. All *gadje* joining a Gypsy family had to become as much like a Gypsy as possible and in every way, including speech, conduct and dress. Gypsies have a particular intonation to their speech I would recognise anywhere. They love to wear brightly coloured clothing and have a love of gold jewellery, particularly gold sovereigns. It was a way of carrying their wealth around with them instead of using banks. The Gypsy gentleman was always very polite to a *gadje* woman, the elderly and young girls, showing them the greatest respect. This integration usually happened easily among the women, and you could hardly tell who was a Gypsy and who was not. My mother did her best but still remained a *gadje*, as she was very much her own person. Nonetheless she was accepted into the family, having left almost all of her *gadje* life behind.

She was only four feet eleven with dark, shoulder-length curls and blue eyes. She took size two shoes on her tiny feet and she often wore my little brother's wellies to go down the garden. She told me a bit about her young life; how she had been brought up on a farm in Devon, and how she had burned her legs in a terrible accident as a child when she had boiling hot jam splashed down her. The doctor said she would be scarred for life, but she had taken to lying on her front under the trees above the house and waving her legs around in the sunshine. In later life her legs showed hardly a mark. She told me stories of the friends she had made and the many little gifts they had given her. She had trained as a nurse before she married. But Mum never looked back, and *we* were her life. I was never really curious about her life before me; there was always plenty to interest me in the here and now.

She truly loved her garden, and if we did not find her in the wagon, that is where she would be. She would look up when we called, her face flushed with her exertions. Her face would light up when she saw us.

'Hello, hello,' she would say, 'come and have a look at my apple tree!'

When people say they commune with nature, I think of my father. He loved all that grew and all creatures that lived, except rats. These he hated so much that he would not even say the word but called them 'long tails'. They ruined so much animal food, took the chickens' eggs and killed the baby chicks, so I grew to loathe them as well. I suppose they must have their place, but I don't know what it could be.

Dad had his own patch of garden, which used to be an old chicken run, so the ground was very fertile. He would walk about in it in the mornings and the evenings, often talking to God about the things that grew. You couldn't call my dad a religious man, by the standards of some; he only went to church for weddings and funerals.

'Only bad people go to church,' he would say. 'The rest got no need.'

He loved to grow things, and knew that they only grew with the Lord's help. He would stand and chat for ages about his vegetables. I used to be quite shocked that he spoke to God in such a familiar way, but now I think he was very blessed. Not that he was a saint, certainly not. When he was being quiet and nice he could charm anyone, but get on the wrong side of him and watch out! We would all get out of his way until he calmed down. He could not read or write, as he had rarely been to school. He could write his own name, but that was all. But he could add long columns of figures in his head in seconds. He was a wonderful mathematician, and I often wished he had taught me but Dad was not a good teacher. He was far too impatient, and was not prepared to sit down long enough.

He was a very stubborn man. All his thoughts ran in straight lines. He was a true and trusted friend to many, and an implacable enemy to many more. He helped many people along the way in his life and trusted them. Very rarely was his trust misplaced, as he was a fairly good judge of character.

One day, a motorist broke down outside our camp. Cars were very rare sixty years ago, and we would only see one or two pass in a day. The man had no money and needed two tyres. At that time my father and his brothers bought and sold scrap cars and metal, so my dad found two good tyres that would fit. Dad let him have the tyres and the man promised to pay him for them next time he passed.

'You've seen the last of that!' my uncles laughed.

'No,' said Dad, ''e said 'e'd pay and 'e will.'

Nearly a year went by, then one summer morning Dad was by the roadside when a car pulled up beside him. Out got a man and approached Dad, pulling out his wallet.

9

'I've come to pay you for the tyres you let me have. Sorry it's been a long time but I live over in Wales, see, and this is the first chance I've had to come over this way.' He smiled apologetically.

'Oh, thanks,' said Dad, casually putting the money in his pocket, 'I knew you'd be back sometime.'

Dad never let anyone forget this, which is why I remember it so well. He was a very trusting man, and seemed happier for it. He was one of life's givers, and nothing made him happier than when he had something to share.

I have a clear memory of myself as a very young child sitting on the wagon floor and opening a brown-paper parcel. Inside was a lovely teddy bear with a growl in his belly and dressed in pink corduroy trousers and a red jacket. In his ear was a sweet little stud. I loved him to bits, and we all played with him over the years, but I think it was me who finally took the silver stud out of his ear. Too late now to worry about what his value might have been; to me he was priceless anyway. Dad also bought me a duck made from Black Watch kilt material. He got it from an ex-soldier who made them. I have it still, and would not part with it for anything.

I can only imagine Granny-in-Town's dismay when Mum married a Gypsy lad the minute she was twenty-one. Nothing was ever said in front of us children, but Granny-in-Town visited our camp only once. I remember it very well. She brought me a lovely present of a silver and white fairy dress complete with a magic wand. I wore it for weeks until it fell apart. Gypsy Granny looked on in disgust after she had left.

"Ee don't want they silly things, Rosie! That silly playin' won't put food in yer belly!'

I took no notice.

'You play while you've got the chance, Rosie!' said Mum. I was only three or four, and never minded Granny's scolds. I also never thought my life was lived in two compartments. I was a Gypsy, and that was that.

Dad never mentioned her at all, but Mum used to visit her once a week on the bus until Granny-in-Town died, alone to start with, but later she took us along. She was a sweet, white-haired old lady, but she could not have been that old as she still worked as a head cook in a posh hotel in town. I had started school before I even saw Granny's house. She worked long hours, and had to stay overnight in the hotel. I still saw her once a week on her day off, as Mum caught the same bus as Granny and they took me to the zoo or to the pictures. Relations must have been strained, as in those days it would have been unthinkable for a *gadje* girl to run off and marry a Gypsy even though the idea was widely romanticised in novels.

Mum's life was very hard after she married my father, but I never heard her reproach him for it. She kept her thoughts and feelings to herself. When we visited Granny-in-Town she always gave us a wonderful tea, all home-made. Other times, we would meet her on the bus to Bristol and she would take us to the zoo for the day or to the pictures in town. This was an occasional treat, and she would always ask us what sweets we would like. Then she would wait patiently while my brothers and I made our choices. Looking back on the many treats Granny-in-Town sent home to us, I realise what a kind person she was. She showed her love for us in everything she did. My mother loved her dearly, and missed her very much when she died, as we all did. Granny told me shortly before she died that no matter how she felt, when she saw my mother coming down the road she knew everything was all right. I remembered this shortly after she died, and told Mum.

'I'm glad you told me that, Rosie,' she said tearfully. 'I have tried to make things right.'

That was all she ever said that gave any indication of what had happened between them, but *she* knew what she meant. So I realised that some aspects of our lives can be hidden from those we love, but perhaps that is just as well. Maybe knowing too much would change our feelings about each other, and sometimes not for the best.

Whenever my mother and father had any money to spare, which was not very often, they seldom agreed on how to spend it. Dad was all for enjoying it on treats that were short-lived but immensely enjoyable, while Mum wanted to spend it on necessary things, with perhaps a little over to save.

One day, having a few shillings to spare, they decided to take me to have my photograph taken by a *real* professional photographer in town. What a treat! I was very small then, and still an only child at this time, so it seemed really special. I was taken to town aboard my dad's old lorry. I always enjoyed a trip into the town in this fashion.

Dad parked the lorry in the centre of town with ease, and we three strolled down the street to the photographer's shop.

However, just before we got there, I spotted a shoe shop selling shiny black wellington boots. Instantly they were all I ever wanted. Well, that was it. I wanted *that* pair of shiny black wellies, and they could not drag me away. Mum explained that she didn't have enough money for the wellies *and* a photograph. I would not move.

They counted the money and discussed the cost as I gazed lovingly at these two vulcanised creations. The wellies cost one shilling and sixpence and the photo would cost two shillings (approximately seventeen pence in total today). It sounded so little, yet every penny was needed. Finally, after some more counting, Mum reasoned that the wellies would be ideal for playing around the yard in, and they gave in. So there I stood, proudly placing each foot down like ready cash all the way to the photographer's.

If Mum and Dad thought all was then peaceful, they were wrong. When we got to the photographer's I would not take the wellies off for the photo. Mum pleaded, Dad begged and the flustered photographer tried to bribe me with a sticky lolly, but to no avail. The boots were on, and they were there to stay as far as I was concerned.

So the photographic evidence shows, for all posterity, me with a mutinous expression, proving what a battle it had been, complete with wellies.

Mum collected the photos a few weeks later and there I was, proudly sporting my shiny black boots. Mum, in a very rare fit of temper, cut the offending footwear from one photo, but another remained intact. Dad decided he liked it and showed it to all, boasting about the fight I had put up, and I slept soundly that night, tucked up in bed, wellies and all.

My mother gave birth to all her children – myself and my three younger brothers, Nelson, Edward and Christoper – at home in our wagon. She saw our doctor probably once or twice at the most with each pregnancy, as doctors cost money. Either the midwife or the district nurse arrived only at the birth and just once after. Most of these women were kind enough, but their attitude showed that they resented looking after Gypsy folk, and one of them was under the influence of drink, which upset my mother a great deal. Mum never drank alcohol, and she felt very frightened at the thought of someone delivering her baby if she was not sober. I was born healthy and strong, as were my brothers Teddy and Chris, but Nelson was born with dislocated shoulders and something wrong with his hip. He was less than two pounds when he was born, smaller than a bag of sugar. After he was born, the midwife spoke very bluntly.

'I'll be surprised if he lasts the night.'

Then she took her drunken self off, leaving my mother to cope as best she could. Mum told me years later that she had burst into tears, not knowing what to do. Just then, Nelson cried. He looked just like a skinned rabbit and she should know, having seen plenty of them in her time. Her heart went out to him and she picked him up and held him to her breast. To her joy, he began to suck. She held him until he fell asleep.

All my aunties helped my mother as much as they could, giving us meals and doing our washing. The midwife visited once more and curtly stated that she was surprised to see the baby still alive. Mum let her go without a word. She was so tired and ill she could not bring herself to speak to 'that woman'.

Mum looked after Nelson without any doctors or nurses visiting, and if he fell ill and Dad was away somewhere, she would have to take him on the bus all the way to the hospital in town. Sometimes she would have to leave him there, going back to see him as often as she could, but it was only my mother's care that enabled him to survive. Mum told me she met much kindness there, but also a lot of prejudice from some of the hospital staff. This went on for years until he went to school, where some teachers and pupils made the poor boy's life a misery.

Nelson grew tall, thin and pale. He got a little browner in the summer and looked a lot healthier, but life was not easy for our Nelson. It was a struggle for him to do the everyday things that other children did so easily, so we made allowances for him and he never let anything stop him. When Uncle Leonard brought his logs home from the woods and stacked them in the yard, we would be in our element, climbing all over them, playing cowboys and Indians and Tarzan of the jungle. These games cost nothing and kept us all strong and healthy, including Nelson.

Mum often asked me to look after the boys while she did the washing or gardening when they were very young. I loved my little brothers, but sometimes found it a bit of a trial looking after them when I had lots of things I would rather do. Yet if one of my cousins wanted to play with the baby or asked to push the pram, I felt very jealous and would not let them near.

My brother Edward, known as Teddy, was loved by all as he was such a beautiful child with his golden curls and big blue eyes. I didn't mind so much looking after him as he was such a good baby. There were six years between us, so in those days I was considered quite old enough to take care of him. Sometimes I became so engrossed in my own thoughts and plans for the rest of the day that I would completely forget he was there. Once or twice I wandered off, oblivious to the sleeping child, until I heard my parents calling me.

'Rosie! Rosie! Where's that gal got to? She's left the baby – anything could have happened to him!'

Then my Gypsy granny would join in.

'Rosie! Rosie! She be off reading somewhere, no doubt. I said no good would come o' they books!'

Quietly, hoping no one would notice, I crept back. They noticed all right.

'That baby could've choked!' Granny scolded. She was really angry. Mum and Dad said no more. If only they could have seen me when I *was* looking after him. I was always worried about him because when he was asleep he used to go so pale I would be terrified that he was dead. I would shake his pram violently. Teddy went from one end of the pram to the other and still wouldn't wake up. Then I would try poking and tickling his little chest until he did wake, proving it by yelling at the top of his voice. That prompted another scolding.

I discovered that I could swing on the handle of his pram, which resulted in poor Teddy being tipped out onto the clinkers. I told no one about this, as I knew the trouble I would be in. I also knew it was not healthy for him and could damage his poor head, so then I became even more afraid he would die and poked the little soul awake even more. Mum always said he was a good sleeper, sleeping right through the night. It was probably due to the fact that I kept him awake most of the day. Poor Teddy was probably exhausted.

My baby brother Christopher was chubby and dark with peachy skin and huge dark eyes. Because he was the baby of the family, we all had to take care of him. The trouble was, he always thought he could do all the things us older ones could. He used to follow us like a puppy and get lost as a result.

He wanted to join in whatever game we were playing, and as young as he was he picked up the rules very quickly. One day he begged us to let him play draughts. No, we decided, he wouldn't be able to understand the game. We let him watch day after day until we finally gave in to his pleading.

'Oh, let him have a go,' I said, 'he'll soon get fed up.'

First we let him lay out the board, which he did perfectly. Then he played us all, one after the other, wiping the board with every one of us! We were all extremely impressed. He had learned to play simply by watching us.

A group of my cousins and I decided we would go across the fields and orchards for the day. We all took bread and cheese and set off. Chris tagged along after us.

'Let me come! Let me come too, our Rosie!'

'No, you're too small. Go on home.'

He kept calling, louder and louder. We were scared Mum might hear us and make us stay home or, worse still, take him with us.

'Shush. Be quiet. We'll take you next time.'

'You said that last time!' he bellowed.

He was only about two and a half, so no way did we want him with us. He screamed and yelled, finally throwing himself down in the dirt kicking his heels in a rage. We tried to run off, afraid that we would be seen. Suddenly his face lit up, and running into the chicken house he gathered up some eggs that Dad had put under a hen to make her broody. Running as fast as his little legs would go, he caught up with us and began pelting us with the rotten eggs. Being so young, most missed their mark except one, which caught Teddy fair and square on the side of the head. The smell was indescribable. I felt sick. We all felt sick. We felt even sicker when my dad saw what had happened. Of course, Christopher was not blamed. He was 'only a baby', Mum said. I was upset. He may have been young but he knew that he shouldn't touch the hen's eggs. Of course, we were not allowed to go anywhere that day, and we had to clean up the rotten eggs. I will never forget the terrible stench. Poor Teddy had to get a bucket of water himself to try and wash the smell out of his hair, but we could still smell it days later. Well, maybe we just thought we could.

After that day we had to take Chris with us almost everywhere. He was a lovely boy but he often got into scrapes.

There were many wheat and hay fields near us, and we loved to play in the long grass but we had to be careful because if there had been any damage Dad would have to compensate the farmer. He named his price and Dad paid it. He was bitter about this because the farmers never paid him compensation when their cows got out and ruined our peas and beans one day.

It was a hot day, and we decided to look for grasshoppers. We thought we would venture around the edges of the field so that would be all right. We were out for some time when I suddenly realised Chris was missing. I felt a pang of fear and my tummy felt hollow.

'Chrissy! Chrissy!' we all shouted. 'Where are you?'

One of my younger cousins used to call Chris 'Kipper' as he couldn't say 'Christopher', so he called 'Kipper!'

We all called until we were hoarse. Where could he be? By this time I was in tears. I suddenly realised how much we all loved him. How could I go back to my mother and father and tell them Chris was lost?

It was getting late. The sun had gone down and the sky was pink and gold but we had no eyes for its beauty. We knew we would have to go home without him. The only thing we could think of was to ask God to help us. None of us had ever set foot inside a church, but we all knew there was a God and that he would help us if we deserved it. So we all stood in a circle, joined hands and solemnly asked God to help us find our Chris.

With a sigh of relief we decided to look a bit more, so we started walking around the edge of the field. Halfway around I noticed the wheat had been disturbed. I pointed silently with a shaking hand at the spot where he might be. A small voice behind me called out, 'It's awright, Kipper! Ise tummin! Ise tummin, Kipper!' and my little cousin raced towards the rustling wheat. There was little Chris sitting and smiling at us sleepily, rubbing his eyes. We hugged him fiercely and took him home as fast as our legs could carry us. We never told our parents what had happened, but my mother looked a bit puzzled when Chris told her: 'Mammy, I went to sleep in the wheat field!'

Granny and Granfer

My grandparents were true travelling Gypsies. They had travelled the length and breadth of the country countless times before settling in two fields and a paddock for the horses in the heart of Somerset. Granny was said to have entered the gates after her purchase and uttered these immortal words: 'This yer be ower ground, and there ain't nobuddy goin' to move we no more!'

And so it was, though many tried over the years, but Granny had perfected the art of dumb insolence from birth and never lost a battle. So Granny and Granfer brought up their large family of twelve children in a wagon and a tent and made a good job of it. My father and his sisters and brothers travelled the roads with Granny. When she bought the land, they all settled there with their families. My father said that he never wanted to travel the roads again. He was thirty-one when he married my mother, and she was twenty-one, so he had been travelling for at least thirty years.

Granny was a true Romany, and looked it. She was tiny with piercing black eyes and a Roman nose. Her hair was silver and wound around her head in two plaits above heavy jet earrings which dangled from her stretched, pierced earlobes. Her family regarded her with the deepest respect, and not a little fear. She was spotlessly clean and used a separate bowl for each job. She would turn in her grave if she could see the all-purpose bowls that we use today. I often wonder if Granny had Jewish blood; she had many Jewish ways.

Granny was small and slim. Most of her clothes were given to her, but she always had her pinnies made by a lady who lived nearby. They were made of black sateen. She had two special ones for best, embroidered with purple feather stitching, and for everyday she had three black sateen pinnies with pale mauve stitching. Whatever clothes she wore, as soon as Granny put on one of her pinnies she looked lovely. On top she wore a tidy coat and always a little brown felt hat with flowers along the brim, and this was kept in place with several large hat pins. I could never watch her pin her hat on as I was convinced the pins were going through her head. When she was ready to go out, she picked up her basket and made sure her roll of money was in her pinny pocket and her snuff box was close to hand and off she would go.

Granny used to take all her grandchildren over the fields with her to pick wild flowers, which we would then sell door to door in nearby villages. We picked baskets of cowslips, primroses and wild orchids which Granny called 'hawkits'. How sad I felt when I realised years later that they would never grow again.

Going out with her basket every day was Granny's job. She brought in a little money and kept in touch with all sorts of people and their way of life. She chatted with everyone she came into contact with, and people were always pleased to talk to her. She would include a bit of fortune-telling if asked, but never gave anyone bad news and sent them away happy. She would tell the young married women that they would soon be having a baby, which pleased most of them to bits. Sure enough, when Granny returned several months later, there would be a row of newly washed nappies on the line. Granny had a good time selling her nappy pins, baby powder and cream.

'How did you know I would be having a baby?' they would ask, incredulous. Granny would tap the side of her nose and smile knowingly.

'That's fer me to know, m'dear. I can't give away they sort o' secrets.'

Afterwards, she laughed as she told us her 'secret'.

'Well, if 'ee just got wed and got no sense, it stands to reason, unless 'ee's unlucky, 'ee'll soon 'ave a baby under yer pinny!'

Many evenings during the winter, we would go over to Granny's place and help her make artificial flowers out of paper. She showed us how to wire them on to small dead branches. When we had made enough, she would melt some coloured wax in an old pan and then quickly dip the flowers in the wax. They used to look beautiful. This was long before the days of plastic or even silk flowers. When Granny took these out to sell in her basket they sold like hot cakes, especially in the houses of the 'gentry', as Granny called them. She would also dip small branches or evergreens in gold or silver paint, which were also very popular.

Granny used to keep her flowers in the wash house tied in bunches. They were steeped in a bath of cold water ready for sale the next day. On one unforgettable day, my cousin Betty was doing some washing when suddenly she was soaked to the skin. My father happened to be passing by and saw that the legs of her dungarees were on fire. He seized the first thing that came to hand – which happened to be the bath of Granny's flowers – and threw it all over her. The force of the water knocked her over. I shall never forget the sight of her flat on her back and covered in daffodils. The flames from the boiler had licked out and set fire to her dungarees. Granny was wild, and shouted at my dad for throwing her flowers over Betty and spoiling them. The fact that Betty could have been burned to death did not enter her head. I thought my father had been very clever and scowled at Granny, earning a clip around the ear from her for daring to be so rude. The old wash house stood for years, and was the site of many shared confidences, hidden tears and quarrels over whose turn it was to use the boiler.

In the autumn, Granny would hand us large wicker baskets and we went gathering sloes and blackberries. We sold the blackberries to a man who came twice a week. He paid us a shilling a pound and we gave this straight to our mothers. It helped pay for our school clothes. We saw nothing odd about this, as money was always tight. Granny made gin with the sloes, which I was told was delicious.

On misty autumn mornings we would get up early and run through dew-wet grass to collect enormous baskets of wild mushrooms. A handful of berries and a freshly picked mushroom would made a tasty and filling breakfast, though I would never eat a raw mushroom if I was alone as I could never quite trust my own judgement. I was afraid that it might be a toadstool pretending to be a mushroom. Granny would show us where to gather the plants she dried and used as herbs and medicines, and we spent hours collecting them. Once home, she would hang them in bunches from racks in the ceiling of the hut. With these, she had a remedy for every ill.

Granny used to keep her medicines and herbs in a little cupboard, and this had to be scrubbed every week. I used to read the labels on the tins and bottles: Friar's Balsam, Slippery Elm, Syrup of Figs and Senna Pods. 'Slippery Elm' set my imagination running. What was it made of? I imagined a huge elm tree with the branches and trunk covered in a slimy substance, but when I peered into the tin it contained only a sort of powder, which had to be made into a drink with hot water. It looked and tasted horrible but Granny swore by it and was always trying to persuade someone or other to take it. We all knew what senna tea was as we often saw it bubbling away on Granny's stove. The smell was awful and it tasted worse, and Granny saw to it that we all had a dose every week without fail. I hated the stuff and begged my mother not to let me take it. None of us needed it in any case, as we had plenty of roughage. We lived on fresh vegetables, apples and any fruit in season. Finally my mother gave in and went over to Granny's with a cup so she could give us our dose in the wagon every Friday night. Granny stared at Mum suspiciously.

'Make sure 'ee do, Mary,' she warned. 'They'll 'ave bad stummics if 'ee don't!'

Mum kept her word, but gave us a much smaller dose than Granny, with a few raisins to take the taste away. When Granny asked her if we had taken our doses she could look her in the eyes and say that yes, we had. I often think we got better in spite of her cures.

I loved the smell of Friar's Balsam, however, with the picture of the fat old friar on the label of the chubby brown bottle. You could work wonders with this lovely smelly stuff. According to Granny, it worked on head colds, congestion of the lungs and many other ailments. Granny did not think it was better than her own herbal potions, but it would do if she was short of herbs or if it was the wrong time of year. Granny was getting older, and she said the cold was getting into her 'poor old bones'.

Granny was never wrong about anything. For instance, she thought she was a wonderful cook. She wasn't. Even as a child I realised this, but she had so indoctrinated her family with this idea that they all thought so as well, and always appeared to enjoy her meals. My mother gave us a varied diet and even made gravy, which Granny thought quite foolish. Granny only made gravy once, when she was looking after us for the day. My parents had gone out and so Granny tried to be kind and made us some gravy to go on our dinner. When it came to the table, she had to cut it into slices before she could put it on our plates. We knew better than to say one word about it, and manfully ate without comment. No one asked for seconds.

It was the same with her stews. They weren't so bad – it was the dumplings that went with them. When she added them to the boiling morass, they sank without trace, only to be discovered later as solid and rock hard as they had gone in, welded to the bottom of the stew pot.

I think my Granny invented one-stage cookery. She boasted that she never weighed anything. The results testified to that. She had a large coal range which she would get really hot while she threw all her ingredients into a large bowl. At least five pounds of flour, and whatever she had in the way of fat, dried fruit and sugar. She would also add a large lump of salt cut from the block. This would then be roughly mixed together with water and a couple of eggs, scraped into any handy container and thrust into the furnace-hot oven. Periodically she would inspect this culinary experiment until she judged it to be ready. This could be anything from ten minutes to half an hour, depending on the size of the tin: of course, it never was cooked properly, but, strangely, smelled delicious. If any of us children were unlucky enough to be around when it was taken out of the oven, we were given a huge slice each and watched closely by a pair of questioning eyes. So we would make appropriate noises to show our delight and approval. If we came across the lump of salt, it was swallowed without a word or grimace.

Her pastry would be made using the same method as her cakes. She never cut the pastry to fit the plate but rolled it out in all directions into a large, rubbery, rough circle shape, then placed it over the plate. Then she rummaged around a bit until all the fruit or whatever contents she was using was in the centre. Then, in a sudden burst of activity, she flapped the pastry edges to the centre until it was several layers thick over the filling. Of course, it was never cooked through and when sliced up was really revolting. We usually tried to make ourselves scarce whenever this 'delicacy' was dished up, but were caught later and offered an oversized piece.

The worst part of this charade was the fact that Granny-in-Town was an excellent cook. Her cakes and pastries just melted in the mouth, and we always had room for more. She often sent down some of these for Sunday tea. Gypsy Granny would fix us with her bright black eyes and demand to know who was the best cook: herself, or Granny-in-Town? Cowards that we were, we always replied, 'Oh, you, of course, Granny! You're the best.' I always felt guilty afterwards, but I knew my other granny would have understood that we had no choice and maybe even chuckled over it.

Granny often asked us to do odd jobs for her, and it never entered our heads to refuse to help her. She was our grandmother, and we deeply respected her. We knew how hard she worked herself so we always agreed to anything she asked of us. The wooden table where she prepared the food was scrubbed white after the supper dishes were washed. Her tea towels were boiled in a bucket of soda water on top of the stove and every night they would blow snowy white on the line. Her dish-cloths got the same treatment. No dirty rags for Granny: they had to be snow white or they would have to be washed again. The only light came from a tilley lamp, which made a loud hissing sound. I was a bit scared of these lamps but they gave a good light and quite a lot of heat. Granny cooked the supper every evening by the light of these lamps on the small stove. What could not be cooked on this would be hung over the camp fire. If the weather was fine, supper would be eaten around this fire. Maybe a bit of meat, always vegetables and 'taters', as Granny called them.

As well as the tilley lamps, we used a Primus stove. This was little more than a camping stove. It had to be started by pouring methylated spirit into a cup-like container, setting it alight and then pumping hard until there was a fierce hissing flame. How we never had an accident with it, I shall never know. I was convinced that at some point the little stove would explode, but it never did. As we had no gas, electricity or running water for many years, we used oil lamps and candles as well for lighting. Finally, after overcoming many bureau-cratic obstacles, Granny had gas installed, which meant gas lighting and a gas cooker. The gas lighting was a wonder to all of us. To turn it on we just had to pull a little chain and then put a match to the gas mantle, then with a pop and a whiff of gas we had light. The trouble was, once the mantle had been lit it became extremely fragile, barely hanging together, so if your hand shook, as it usually did, the match would go right through the mantle and it would crumble as delicately as a dandelion clock. Then there would be grumbles while everyone hunted for a new mantle. I don't think this innovation lasted too long as most people were able to move on to electricity, but I think we had gas lighting longer than most as we had no choice. This made life a lot easier for everyone, and once the principle of how a thermostat worked was understood, Granny got a gas iron. When, later, I mentioned this gas iron at school, no one believed me. They could not understand how it worked. From what I can remember, the iron was attached to the gas supply and then turned on with a little tap. The iron itself consisted of a base plate and a top plate with a gap in the middle. Around the edge of the base plate was a row of little burners. Once the gas was switched on and the burners lit, the flames could be adjusted. It was difficult to get the flame just right, neither too low or the flame would go out, nor too high or the flames would lick around your hands, causing whoever was doing the ironing to let out a loud scream and drop the iron. If you were anywhere near during this process you would hear, 'Ouch!' (scream), a loud thud as the iron was dropped and the hissing of gas as the flames blew out. This was followed by complaints and muttering about who had the matches last. This could be quite entertaining for the onlooker, but very annoying for the one ironing. I am sure these irons were very dangerous, but despite burned knuckles, they were used for a long time, taking the place of the heavy flat irons that we used to heat up on the range. In many ways, the modern kitchen appliances Granny used were more of a hindrance to her, and she often resorted to her old kitchen range in preference to the gas cooker which she would forget to light.

One day, last summer, I was walking down a country road when the smell of paint wafted towards me on a warm summer breeze. At once I was six years old again, watching Granny stirring her paint. This was a lengthy annual ritual. She would go to her paint cupboard and drag out several rusty tins, prise the lids off and peer suspiciously into each one to see if it was still usable. Then she poked her nose down inside to smell it. I don't know why she did this, but I always expected her nose to come out dripping with paint. It never did. When she was satisfied with her collection, she would tip the contents of some of the tins into the largest and stir it with a stick until it was blended into a uniform ghastly brown.

This was followed by much movement and scraping of tables and other furniture, which would all end up outside the hut. The hut was quite big, and contained some large pieces of furniture, some of which would have been worth a small fortune these days, had they survived in their original state. But Granny never left them like that. She arranged them in a neat row, picked up her brush and tin and started to slap it on. She never prepared the furniture in any way, just waited for the first hot day and painted everything in sight, adding more layers to those already there, like the rings on a tree. She only took a short time over it, and when she had finished, she would lean back proudly, wiping her brow as she surveyed her accomplishments.

All was left to dry in the hot sun. It never quite dried, though, and for months afterwards we would discover paint stains on legs and clothes. My aunties always had paint-stained knuckles after opening cupboard doors and forgetting to use their fingertips. By the time it was really dry, it was time for Granny to start all over again.

Granny found *gadje* ways hard to bear, and was not afraid to speak her mind on the subject loud and often. When she heard that a well-to-do *gadje* family in the village were having a bathroom installed with an indoor lavatory, she was utterly disgusted.

'Fancy 'avin' a lavatory *in the 'ouse!*' she remarked. 'The best place fer they is at the bottom o' the garden. They don't want stinkin' things like that inside!'

Maybe she was right. Our soil toilet was housed in a little corrugated-iron shed at the far end of the camp. It consisted of an old, cut-down oil drum with a hinged wooden plank attached with a hole cut out in the middle. Soil and sawdust were placed inside and a bucket of the same with a small shovel placed nearby. A few squares of newspaper hung from a rusty nail on the back of the door, and that was all that was needed. At night, a pot was used if necessary.

The *gadje* wives – my mother included – listened, but could not reply when their husbands stood up for their mother in any disagreement. On the other hand, Granny would often support the *gadje* wives if there were any problems within the marriage. For example, when my parents were first married, my father, who was not a mean man, doled out housekeeping money in miserly amounts to my mother. Mum, not knowing any better either, managed the money with great difficulty but never complained. Granny saw her handing back some change to my father after buying a few groceries and took my mother to one side.

'Don't be foolish, gel! Never give 'im any change back. Keep it in yer pocket. If 'e thinks 'ee don't need it, 'ee won't get any more!'

Mum realised she was being foolish and followed Granny's advice. My father did not notice his change was never returned, and life was a bit easier for her. Granny often gave wise advice, and helped us all in lots of ways, showing us how to find the best nuts and wild fruit, which helped our mothers as it was all free.

Granny's place was a very large chicken house made into one large bedroom and a kitchen-cum-living room. It was a great improvement on the tent and wagon she had previously been living in. A chicken house does not sound very homely, but when Granny had scrubbed it and painted the outside her favourite shade of brown, it was all that Granny desired. She put linoleum on the floor, added a scrubbed pine table and a beautiful range that was kept glowing summer and winter. Sometimes Granny would let us play cards in front of it in the winter. Seven-card brag was our favourite, and we would play for hours, chatting and laughing, sometimes cheating, but always comfortable in each other's company. Sometimes Granny or one of our uncles would tell us to be quiet if we got too noisy.

One day, Granny had a letter from the council demanding that she take the chicken house down as it was now a home, and only movable dwellings were allowed on her land. Over the months, letter followed letter. My mother read them to Granny, as she had never learned to read. She told her that Granny needed a solicitor, but Granny refused and ignored all the letters. Then men came from the council. Granny politely invited them in and gave them each a cup of tea, liberally laced with whisky. After several cups of this, they neither knew nor cared what Granny did. They sent more men. Granny fed them tea and behaved as though they weren't there. Finally another letter came saying Granny could keep the chicken house! Well, Granny always knew she would.

Uncle Alfie drove the old lorry into town on a Saturday, and Mum would go in with Granny. She would put on her best hat with the big felt flowers, her best pinny and her good black shoes with the slits cut out of the side to give her bunions room. With her best coat on, she would be ready. After calling my mother, she sat in the old wooden rocking chair calling to my uncle at the top of her voice.

'Alfie! Alfie, I'm ready! Is the conveyance to hand?'

I cannot think where she learned this grand word to describe the old lorry, but it sounded very strange coming from the lips of this old Gypsy woman.

Alfie was a lovely man with sailor-blue eyes that twinkled in his oily black face, and a very rough voice that scared little children until they got used to him. He never married or had children of his own, but he often thought of us when we were little. If he saw that someone had thrown out toys for the dustman, he reasoned that they were unwanted and brought them home for us.

Granfer slept in the bedroom which he shared with my Uncle Alfie. Alfie's bed was a double, Granfer's a high old hospital bed. He suffered with bronchitis for the last fifteen years or so of his life and could not do any heavy work, although he still bought and sold at the markets and sale rooms, but Granny went out with her basket most days. She was a very tiny person, about seven stone in weight and about five feet tall, so I was amazed one day when I tried to pick up her basket. It was so heavy! Yet she carried it for five or six hours at a time. When she sold holly and mistletoe at Christmas, she must have been worn out by the end of the day, yet she never showed it.

Each day, when she had sold everything, she filled her basket with groceries from the proceeds and always brought Granfer back a treat. A packet of snuff, a small bottle of whisky or cough drops. She seemed to enjoy giving these small gifts to the man she called 'my Edwin'. He would smile and thank her as if she was a queen, and she was, in his eyes. Sometimes my uncles would chide her for spending her hard-earned money in this way, but her ears were deaf to them.

She never felt that she was wasting her money on the little gifts she bought for Granfer. She enjoyed the giving as much as he enjoyed the receiving of them. Granny was not a woman who showed her feelings easily, and she certainly did not go in for lots of hugs and kisses, so a small bottle of whisky, an ounce of snuff or a box of cough sweets meant a lot to Granfer.

'Thank 'ee, Mary Ann,' he would say in his gentle way, giving her a smile. Granny would say nothing, but the way she looked at Granfer was enough.

'Sit thee down 'ere, my Edwin,' she would coax, putting his chair near the fire and placing his mug of tea within his reach. Granfer would put a drop of whisky in his tea and, leaning back with a contented sigh, would say: 'Well, me dear, I wouldn't call the King me uncle!'

Picking up the poker, he would jab at the coals in the fire. That was the one thing that was guaranteed to drive Granny mad if anyone else did it, but she always turned a blind eye if 'my Edwin' did it. When Granfer suffered a lot from bronchitis during the last years of his life, Granny looked after him, doing her very best to keep him in the warm.

'Nay, Mary Ann,' he would chide, 'let me be! I'll get about while I got the chance. I'll be a long time dead!'

'Don't 'ee say that, my Edwin. I just be tryin' to look after 'ee.'

Granfer went his own way, though, still going to the market every week and bringing back all sorts of interesting things. We could hardly wait for the cart to stop before we would start rummaging about in the boxes to see what treasures we could find.

My granfer – what can I tell you about him? I would need a dozen books to do him justice. He was tall, thin and as brown as the leather on the horses' saddles. His hair was silver, with a kiss curl in the middle of his forehead. He wore an old brown trilby hat on the back of his head, and to me looked very dashing. He was a quiet man, but very kind and loving. Granny was his heart's delight. I know this because I often heard him tell her so. He deserved our respect and he got it. He used to call me 'my pretty' and 'my flower', and that used to make me feel very special.

When I was very young, I imagined that God must look like Granfer, because his face was full of love, just like the pictures of Jesus I had seen on my Aunt Betsy's wall. We all loved him very much, but despite this we teased him sometimes.

My brother put a firework under his chair once, just as he was dozing. He leaped up as though he had been shot and chased us, waving his walking stick, but we did not fear him as we knew he would never harm us.

'Mary Ann, Mary Ann!' he would shout to Granny. 'These varmints are up to their tricks again!'

Granny was the one we had to avoid. She had a firm belief that Satan made work for idle hands, and so made sure we always had something to do.

Early in spring and summer, Granfer would get up and make a camp fire. Then he would fill the old black kettle, put it on the hook to boil and the blackened frying pan would be filled with yesterday's leftover potato and cabbage with a nice bit of fatty bacon and sliced apple. That would be his breakfast. Then he would set to whittling his pegs. Sometimes he would carve wooden flowers. They sold very well at the markets. I liked his flower baskets best. He would cut the thickest briars and remove the thorns, and use these to form a basket on a flat wooden base with a handle of twisted withies. Then he placed a clump of primroses or cowslips inside, and they would look so pretty! He was very deft with his fingers.

Granfer regarded every man as equal, good and decent. As a Gypsy gentleman, he had no fear of speaking to anyone he met in his daily life. He had travelled from Cornwall with Granny to our small village, but once settled he never travelled far; he rarely went further than the surrounding villages. But then, he would never say he travelled. Oh, no. Granfer *voyaged*.

Whenever he spoke of where he had been that day, he would say, 'I voyaged over to see old Jim 'oday.'

Granfer had a bit of a naughty side, however. Once he got on a crowded bus, smelling as usual of snuff, whisky and cough sweets. The haughty lady he sat next to moved away from him with a killing look. Granfer promptly offered her a cough sweet. She turned her head away, curling her lip. Granfer glanced from her to the cough sweets sorrowfully. By now, everyone on the bus had noticed Granfer.

His face brightened in sudden thought.

'Aah! I know what 'ee wants, my maid!'

Reaching deep into the pocket of his old coat, he pulled out a half-bottle of whisky. Unscrewing the top, he lifted it to his lips and took a deep drink, gently burping several times. Then he wiped off the top with his snuff-stained hanky, gently bowed his head and offered her the whisky bottle. White-faced with horror and disgust, she pushed the bottle away, spilling some in the process.

'Never mind, my maid,' says he, screwing back the lid. 'Take it 'ome with 'ee and drink it on thy own in peace and quiet!'

So Granfer's life was full of small voyages, which he loved to tell us about, sitting by the fire, all the while combing his hair into a neat kiss curl.

Granfer loved his horses. They were treated like his own children. Their coats gleamed in the sun; their harness brasses sparkled and shone. He plaited their manes with coloured ribbons, harnessed them up to the red and silver cart and then went off for most of the day. We children never knew exactly where he went, but his breath always smelled strongly of cough sweets when he returned.

When Granfer painted his cart red and silver, we all gathered around to watch. We would have loved to have had a go ourselves, but Granfer would not trust us with a paint brush. As it was, we crept closer and closer until our noses nearly touched the new paint.

'Step back a bit, or go 'way!' said Granfer.

We stepped back, but were soon elbowing each other out of the way again.

'Git back a bit, 'ee varmints! Give me elbow room!'

He still put up with us, and when the paint had dried he got out an old cardboard box full of colourful ribbons and fancy, shiny brasses and started to decorate his cart. When he was sure he was finished, he stepped back the better to see his handiwork. He waved to beckon us towards him.

'What do 'ee think, chillun? Is it good enough to show?'

'Oh, yes, Granfer!' we shouted. 'It be lovely, Granfer!'

Granfer smiled with pride, and taking out his cough sweets, gave one to each of us. We did not really like the taste, but we accepted gratefully.

Granfer was off to the horse fair to look at the young, unbroken colts and perhaps win a prize for the best-dressed horse and cart. Billy Pony was groomed until he shone, and his mane and tail plaited with coloured ribbons. Sometimes Granfer would win a rosette and a few shillings, but also it was a nice day out for him. He would meet up with many old friends and bring them back to the camp for a cup of tea and a drop of whisky. They would talk and laugh long into the night. I could hear their voices until very late, borne along on the night air.

Sometimes these old men and boys would still be there in the morning, still talking over old times and sharing Granfer's breakfast around the camp fire. Granny would be out there as well, enquiring about their wives and children. You never heard these men say a bad word about their wives. Gypsy men looked upon their wives and children as an extension of themselves, and praised them to the skies, each man outdoing the other. To tell the truth, the wives were their husbands' right arms and worked as hard as they did. While she talked, Granny would be packing her withy basket full to the brim with bits of lace, ribbons, brushes, heather, pins, needles and everything that people would want.

Sometimes, when Granny came home, more of Granfer's mates were there and maybe half a dozen or more unbroken colts. We children were told to keep well away from these colts, as we made them nervous. They were not used to being near people, let alone unruly children, so for once we knew we had to keep quiet. Granfer used to break these colts in for the British Army during both wars. We would watch him in the field when he had got to the stage of 'gentling' them on a long tether, then he would shorten it very gradually until he was close enough to put a blanket on the colt's back. Next, he would be able to place a light saddle, then a heavier one until at last he could sit on the horse's back and trot down the field. We thought it was amazing that Granfer could do this. I felt sorry for these poor animals when I learned that they only lasted a short time in battle. It seemed such a waste of these beautiful creatures.

Granfer used to visit all the markets and with his horse, Billy Pony, and brightly painted cart he was well known in the villages and towns round about. He would buy horses and unbroken colts, spending hours breaking them in to the saddle and harness.

It was a treat then to help with the horses. First we would unbuckle the harnesses, and next give them a rub down and a good brush. Finally we would give them a bucket of fresh water and a bag of oats. When they had rested for a while, Granfer let them loose in the paddock. What fun they had! They ran and rolled in the lush grass like children on a beach. Billy Pony would return to Granfer to snuffle in his pockets and blow in his ear.

'They allus comes back in the end,' he would say. 'If you lets 'em go, they allus comes back.'

When my brother Nelson was five years old, Granfer took him to the market for a treat. As usual, Granfer stopped at the inn for a bite and a glass of cider. This time he gave my brother a glass too, which he drank before falling into a drunken stupor. When Granfer arrived home, my brother fell off the cart and staggered glassy-eyed and giggling into his mother's arms and slept the rest of the day away, and most of the next.

One winter, Granfer brought home a goose from the market – a very old goose, as it turned out. Granny dutifully cooked it for hours and hours. When she tried to carve it, however, no impression could be made upon it, so tough had it become. Granfer watched as Granny sawed away at the old bird ineffectually until at last he got up with a sigh and tore it limb from limb. We were all given a piece, but it was like rubber and could not be chewed or swallowed even though we tried. Even the bits given to the dogs and the cat were sniffed and ignored. Granfer would not be beaten, saying it was the best goose he had ever tasted. He sat chewing for what seemed like hours as we watched, waiting for him to swallow the inedible fowl. Finally finishing his portion, he patted his belly in feigned satisfaction, but he never bought a goose again. He did bring back a sack of cabbages, though, and was quite put out that Granny saw fit to add meat and potatoes to the meal as he felt that the cabbages would be sufficient.

'Mary Ann,' he said, 'why 'ee be cookin' tatties when I brought 'ee all they greens?'

Granny told him what he could do with all they cabbages, and the subject was never mentioned again.

He used to buy lots of furniture, beautiful pieces that would fetch a good price now. Granny kept some of the pieces, which she promptly painted brown, but one piece in particular stands out in my memory; a strange and haunting memory, but absolutely true. It was a beautiful cheval-style mirror, about five feet tall, curved at the top and supported on a pedestal with about two inches of space underneath. I stood and gazed into it, noticing my messy hair and grazed knees, when suddenly from beneath the mirror slid a little foot in a shiny black shoe with three buttons on the side and snowy white socks. As I stared, another small foot slid beside it. I couldn't understand it. All I knew was that it wasn't mine. My scruffy sandals and fawn-coloured socks could in no way compare with these delightful creations. I looked behind the mirror. No one there. I looked back at the front. There were the two tiny feet, not moving, side by side. I called my uncle to look, but he wouldn't come.

'It's only your reflection!' he called back. I ran to tell my mother and she said the same. But they weren't my feet. The whole episode remains unexplainable to this day, but I have never forgotten it.

Sometimes the yard was very quiet, with everyone out and about and just a few of us young ones left behind.

Granfer would sit in his armchair in front of the red-hot stove, curling his kiss curl with his index finger, making sure it was dead centre of his forehead, all the while humming or singing softly to himself. I would sit opposite, roasting-hot behind the stove, listening to Granfer while he arranged his hair. I remember feeling a blissful peace in those times. Granfer was a quiet man. Even when he shook his stick at us and called us 'varmints', his eyes still laughed at us. He enjoyed our childish ways, and we in turn enjoyed his company, with all the love and respect we could give a real Gypsy gentleman.

Family Life

When Granny bought her 'bit o' ground', as she called it, I was only a baby. My mother told me later that Granny bought it in late 1937, and I was born in February 1938. The land was divided into two fields. One half of one field was used to grow vegetables to sell, and the other half was for our own food. The rest of the land was where we lived.

To the immediate left of the five-bar gate as you went in was where Aunt Betsy and Uncle Leonard lived with their oldest daughter Violet and Lavinia, their baby girl. They had a wagon and a small wooden hut and lean-to. Aunt Betsy made it look like a little palace; she was always cleaning. She kept her lead crystal and Crown Derby ornaments on display on a high shelf that ran all around the main room, which was a kitchen and living space combined with a curtained area at the back for a bedroom. Gypsies love beautiful things, and can easily recognise the good from the bad. Often the monetary value does not come into it, and so they treasure things for many years, taking great care of them. Most of Aunt Betsy's things were collected when she went out hawking with her basket on her arm. Maybe goods would come in exchange for something she had for sale, such as a load of logs or some plants.

'That be a pretty pot,' Aunt Betsy would remark as she stood in someone's porch. ''Ow much would 'ee take fer 'e?'

The usual reply would be, 'Oh, my mother only gave thruppence or sixpence for that. It's no good.'

'Well, I'll give 'ee three bunches o' daffs fer 'e if yer likes,' she might say. A quick nod, and the deal was done. Some would not realise how much items had increased in value over sixty or seventy years. To give them credit, my aunt and uncle would always give good value in logs, baskets or pegs, so both sides were happy.

Aunt Betsy was a bit of a mixture, sometimes good and sometimes not so good. She could be very funny, and made us laugh without meaning to. She was generous in many ways, insisting that you have something whether you wanted it or not. She loved her garden, and competed with Mum and Granny to see who was the best gardener. What really made us laugh, though, was the little pantomime she performed every morning during the summer.

Before everyone was up, or so she thought, her door opened and out came Betsy in her old working clothes and covered by her wrap-around pinny. She would look around furtively, making sure no one was watching, and then tiptoe up to her beautiful sunflower. She reached up, smoothing the delicate petals, and then ran her finger down its stem, removing any dead material. Then, stepping back, she lifted up the hem of her pinny, curtsied low and said, 'Good morning, Your Majesty!'

She would bow her head for a few more seconds before going inside to begin her day. Of course, everyone knew she performed this little ritual, and she did so for many years. We never knew why, and we certainly would not have asked her. She was a woman of many parts.

When Granny was still using the tent as her kitchen, Aunt Betsy used to scrub the floor and table until they were snowy white. Aunt Betsy was as keen on using herbs as Granny, and used them for every ill. She usually looked really well, whatever the reason was. One winter, she had a hacking cough. Granny told her to sit down near the stove and put a bowl of very hot water on the table and stirred in plenty of Friar's Balsam.

'Lean over, our Betsy, and put this towel over yer 'ead,' Granny ordered. Aunt Betsy did this willingly, and sat under the towel for ten or fifteen minutes, inhaling the steam, and then got up.

'That feels tons better!' she exclaimed.

On getting up, she somehow managed to knock the Friar's Balsam bottle over and it smashed onto the floor, making a terrible mess. Aunt Betsy was very annoyed with herself.

'Now, look at the mess! I'll 'ave to scrub that danged floor all over again.'

'Don't be silly, our Betsy!' said Granny. ''Ee's just this minute scrubbed this floor. Just wipe it over with a clean floor cloth.'

'No, it's gone under the stove. It won't take any longer to do it properly.'

With that, she put all the chairs, the bread hamper and the rugs outside. Granny looked on with a sigh. She could never stop Aunt Betsy once she had made up her mind to do something. On the stove was a large saucepan full of boiling tea towels.

'I'll leave the tea towels. They can keep on boiling.'

'Well, turn 'em down a bit,' Granny suggested, and left her to it. She did not see what happened next. Outside, we could hear Aunt Betsy scrubbing and humming away to herself. Mum came down the wagon steps to get me for my breakfast. She put a bibbed pinny on me and gave me my baby mug. I could not have been any more than about three years old. Suddenly we heard a tremendous crash and the most blood-curdling of screams. I jumped out of my skin, and dropped my little mug of milk. My little dog Tiny lapped it up as fast as she could. She was not one to miss an opportunity.

Everyone rushed to see what had happened, and we children were pushed aside in the fray. I could just see a glimpse of Aunt Betsy lying still on the floor, her back and shoulders covered with steaming cloths. She must have been unconscious with the pain. Everyone seemed to be shouting and screaming, which I found extremely frightening. Granny tried to pull the clothes from her body.

'Fetch me a bit o' butter, quick!' she demanded.

'No, don't use butter,' Mum argued, 'use cold water!' She grabbed a couple of towels, ran to the bucket of cold water in the wash house and plunged them in. Then she pushed her way past the gathering crowd of curious family and draped them across Aunt Betsy's back, in spite of Granny's protests about butter being best for burns. Luckily Mum's nursing training stood her in good stead.

'Get 'er in the lorry!' shouted Uncle Alfie, as Aunt Betsy started to come round, moaning in pain. 'We'll get 'er to 'ospital quick!'

I started to whimper as I could sense the panic in everyone's voices. Mum came over and picked me up.

'There, there. She'll be all right now, don't you worry, Rosie.'

They managed to rush her to Weston General, about nine miles away, but Aunt Betsy was very badly scarred across her back and arm.

She was always cleaning. Years later, she cut an artery in her wrist when she was cleaning out her fish tank. She nearly died then. I thought she must have had nine lives, like a cat.

Once, my brother Nelson saw some rubbish in a side street when we were in town when we were out with Mum.

'Aunt Betsy would soon clean this up, wouldn't she, Mammy?' he remarked.

'She certainly would!' Mum agreed.

While her home was spotless, she usually looked a wreck, mainly because she was always scrubbing or polishing something. The pinny she wore did not protect her from the billowing dust as she worked busily, sweeping here, scouring there, until she was covered in dust and dirt from head to toe. When she was satisfied that everything was gleaming, she would heat two kettles full of water, pour them into a large bowl and scrub herself as vigorously as she had cleaned her home.

She would then put on clean clothes and a dab of lipstick, and my cousin Carol would brush her fair hair into a French pleat; and there Aunt Betsy would be! It was as if someone had waved a magic wand and she could have passed for any lady in the land.

She looked wonderful when she went into town with Uncle Leonard; they made a handsome couple. Heads would turn, as Uncle Leonard looked like an attractive Italian, dark with a small moustache. He worked very hard and looked after his family well by buying large tracts of woodland and sawing up the dead trees into logs with a circular saw. He was missing fingers on both hands because of leaving them on the logs too long, and they were whipped off instantly, but he seemed to manage quite well. He sold the logs from door to door and became very well known in the town. He also sold moss for baskets, which he collected in the woods.

Sometimes he would get out his old wind-up gramophone and his scratchy records and play them. We loved to hear the old songs, and Slim Whitman was my personal favourite. When he sang 'Rose Marie', I pretended he was singing to me. It would be getting dark by the time Uncle Leonard put his records away, but we children had a wonderful time dancing around the yard. We felt like real dancers.

'I'm doin' the rumba!' Violet would declare. It wasn't, but we didn't care.

If anyone was misnamed, it was my cousin Violet. She was far from a shrinking violet! She was more like a beautiful exotic poppy, completely extrovert and full of life and laughter. I thought she was very pretty. Her blue-black hair hung to her waist, plaited neatly by her mother and tied with blue or red ribbons. Her lovely big brown eyes reminded me of the centres of soft brown pansies, but would flash with fire if she were ever in a temper. Her skin was like a peach, and in summer would be as brown as a berry. To top it all she had a ravishing smile that showed two rows of pearly teeth. Yes, I thought her perfect, but in spite of being so fond of her, I envied her. She was always so generous and kind, though, so the feeling didn't last long. I was, and still am, very fond of all my cousins, but we two were especially close and the best of friends. Violet was more like a sister to me, and we seldom fell out. If we ever did we soon made it up again.

Most days we played together, competing in everything, such as who could draw the best. It turned out to be Violet in the long run, as even today she sells many examples of her artwork, which is very beautiful. I simply could not draw or paint. On the other hand, she couldn't tell stories or write them as I could, but she was excellent at describing things she had seen.

Her family were a bit better off than mine, as her father didn't drink or smoke as mine did. So at least once a week she went into town to the pictures. On her return we would run off to a quiet place and, sitting cross-legged, she would recount the film she had seen from beginning to end in glorious Technicolor. She was a very clever mimic, and would add all the voices and actions. It was almost as good as going to see the film myself. Even now I sometimes think I've seen a film on

TV and then realise I've only seen it through Violet's eyes.

Granny had a beautiful crystal ball which was kept covered by a silk shawl and hidden in a cupboard. Rummaging through this cupboard once, my cousin Violet and I found it. We spent ages peering into it, trying to see our futures. We never saw anything, of course, but I pretended to.

'I can see *you*, Vi!' I breathed.

'What? What can you see?' she pleaded, craning over to see.

'You are . . . cutting your hair into a fringe and . . . and . . .' I paused solemnly.

'What? Tell me!' she urged, searching my face in nervous anticipation.

'You are shaving your eyebrows off!' I pronounced emphatically, my eyes avoiding hers so that I would not fall into convulsive laughter. Never one to be put in second place, she at once ran to the dressing table and began to shave off her right eyebrow. I stopped her, and we both gazed into the mirror in horror.

'Quick! Get some soot from the range!' I cried, with sudden inspiration. We tried to draw it back in, but our efforts were in vain: her mother noticed it at once and I was in the doghouse.

When Violet was little, Aunt Betsy and Uncle Leonard took her out with them to deliver logs one day. Aunt Betsy told the very posh lady of the house that Violet was very good and would not touch any of her beautiful flowers. The lady, with somewhat bad grace, allowed Violet to stay in her garden while her parents stacked the logs in the shed at no extra charge. When they had finished, they went to collect their perfect child, only to find her sitting on the manicured lawn surrounded by dozens of daffodil and tulip heads. Violet had single-handedly beheaded almost every plant in the garden. Stunned, they stood rooted to the spot. Even the posh lady was speechless. Only Violet was truly happy, sitting in the spring sunshine and grinning all over her face.

Aunt Betsy and Uncle Leonard exchanged knowing glances. They knew they could not charge for the logs, almost three months' supply plus free stacking. Silently they cleared up the flower heads and stood before the posh lady with their hands full. She made no attempt to take them, so Aunt Betsy poured them into her up-turned pinny and muttered, 'Sorry. Very sorry.' They collected their wayward daughter, still smiling and now waving at the stony-faced lady, and got up into the lorry. They never returned, but on passing by later in the spring, they noticed that the garden was ablaze with colour, obviously having been replanted.

Some time later, it came to my mother's ears that the posh lady had dined out for many months on the story of the little Gypsy girl who had destroyed her lovely garden, and then with a wink and a laugh recounted how she had come off best with a season's supply of free logs!

Strangely, several years later, Aunt Betsy and Uncle Leonard received an official-looking envelope. Betsy saw it first, and took it to my mother for her to read it to her. It was from a solicitor on behalf of the posh lady.

'You have been bequeathed . . .' Mum gasped as she read on. 'She's left you three hundred pounds, Betsy!'

'Well I never!' Betsy exclaimed, sitting down hard. 'She must've liked our Vi'lit!'

Granfer Smith (Violet's granfer) played his accordion and sang love songs to his wife Nellie. She was immensely fat, and always wore Scottish kilts, but she still tripped the fandango and we all clapped her at the end, never so much as sniggering. We accepted her as she was. She was adored by her husband George, who had the same-size frame as a jockey, weighing about seven stones. He was always composing love songs for her and singing them to her, accompanied by his accordion. Some of them were very clever and beautiful. They were never written down and I only remember one, unfortunately.

> Why must we part like this Nell?
> Why must we part this way?
> Who's it to be, him or me
> Don't be afraid to say . . .
> If everything's over between us
> Don't ever pass me by,
> For you and me, friends will be
> For the sake of days gone by.

Nellie would always wipe a tear from her eye after this refrain. 'Oh, Jarge,' she would sigh. Granfer Smith's name was George, but she always called him *Jarge*. It suited him very well. He wore checked trousers, a brown and cream shirt, a brown 'weskit' and a trilby hat. He would go to the horse fairs, and usually had a horse or two for sale. He also had a dog, who loved him and hated everybody else. I lived in fear of that dog, and although it never harmed any of us, I was not sorry when it finally died.

Aunt Nellie had an unusual turn of phrase. She would occasionally ask us to get some shopping for her, and I always giggled when she asked for 'a pound of mar-tresses (tomatoes) and a pound of sosengers' (sausages). She used to get me or my mother to write letters for her. Mostly they were addressed to her daughter, who trav-elled around the country, so the address often went thus: to Elder (Hilda), by the pub or post office (or any other landmark), followed by the name of the town or village. I never knew if Hilda ever got these missives, but I was happy to do it.

One other peculiarity she had was that she had an extra finger on each hand, but it never seemed to bother her. It did not seem to interfere with the use of her hands, with which she very deftly plaited her hair, bunched flowers or cooked. Her hair was long, black and very greasy, as she did not wash it very often, which made it easier to manage, I suppose. She had several chins, which merged into a very fat neck. Her face was as round as the moon and full of dimples. Strangely, her face was charming, with many changing expressions. She was always smiling, her face creasing up like a deflated balloon, and her laugh was infectious. Once she started, we all joined in. In late August or early September she would pop over to our wagon to see my mother.

'Come over 'ome later on, Mary, I want you to measure me fer me kilt.'

My mother knew that was the greatest event in Granny Smith's year.

'All right, Nellie, but you know how long it will take, don't you?'

Nellie nodded.

'Don't worry. I'll get rid of Jarge fer a bit. I can't have him peeking at me in me smalls!'

The thought of that scene was hilarious, and Mum could not stop laughing when she told us later.

'Smalls? There's enough material in Nellie's drawers to clothe a small village!'

She went over to Nellie's later, with three or four measuring tapes and a notebook and pencil to record Nellie's measurements. Mum had kept a record of these for many years in the same notebook, and I found it very interesting to look back through the pages to see how Nellie had got larger and larger over the years, so large, in fact, that she had to have her clothes especially made. As a result, she could only afford a few garments as it was very expensive. The kilt was Nellie's pride and joy. When I asked her once how much it cost, she told me, 'A hundred pounds!' but she may have been exaggerating. So, Mum measured her and off she went to the tailor with her dimensions and the money she had saved hard all year. For the next few weeks she gave us all a blow-by-blow account of her new kilt and the various fittings she had been to. Finally, on the first day of the New Year, she treated us to a showing of the wonderful garment.

'It's not too soon fer a new one!' she declared as she stepped and turned before us all. This was true, as the old one, which she had worn daily for a whole year without washing or cleaning it, was as rotten as a pear. We could not even see the original pattern on the material. Nellie's kilt was a real Scottish kilt in her favourite tartan, made with leather straps, huge safety pins and pleated all around except for the flat panel at the front. As large as Nellie was, she still looked amazing in her hand-made kilt. Why a kilt? I shall never know. Perhaps she felt comfy in it, as she could let the waist out as her girth expanded and she never had to give any thought to what she would wear each day.

Another favour she asked of my mother was to trim her hair. I knew Mum hated doing this as Nellie's hair was so greasy, but Nellie knew that Mum would not let her down.

'Cut me bit o' hair fer me, Mary?' she begged. Mum would try to get out of it with some excuse or other, but Nellie would not give up.

'Go on, gel, you'm a good cutter!'

'But Nellie, I haven't got any sharp scissors.'

'Don't 'ee worry, gel, I got some yere. Jarge used 'em the other day to dock the puppy's tail.'

Mum said that after, she felt sick at the thought. The little spaniel still had his tail bandaged. The scissors looked clean enough, but Mum said that the thought of using the same scissors that had been used to cut the puppy's tail off made her feel ill, and she voiced these feelings to Nellie. The scissors were huge and a bit rusty, but Nellie insisted on washing them in boiling water.

'Don't 'ee worry, gel,' Nellie soothed, 'they can't hurt hair! They be all right!'

So Mum would sit Nellie outside, on the largest chair she could find, put a towel round her shoulders and set to.

'How much off, Nellie?' Mum would ask.

'Not much.'

'Well, how much?' Mum persisted. Mum knew Nellie was very fussy about the length of her hair.

'Well, just start cuttin' an' I'll tell 'ee as yer goes along,' Nellie suggested. Mum sighed, and started to snip across Nellie's back in a straight line, quarter-inch by quarter-inch at a time. Finally she would stand up straight.

'That's enough, Nellie.'

'Thanks, Mary,' Nellie agreed. She could see Mum had had enough. Nellie then combed her greasy locks over her face and divided it into six sections, which she braided into plaits. Then she rolled these into circles and skewered them to her head with hairpins. It looked very odd, but strangely very 'Nellie'. She would admire herself from every angle, quite taken with her own appearance, and kept going back and looking into her mirror. Then she donned her new kilt and a clean blouse.

'Are you going out, Nellie?' Mum asked.

'Oh, no,' she replied, folding her hands into her lap,

'I'm just sittin' 'ere in me chair, an' when Jarge comes 'ome, 'e'll see me straight off. 'E likes me to dress up.'

Mum thought that once a year was not much for Jarge to get excited about. Just as she was leaving, Jarge arrived. He tied up his old horse to the fence and then, looking up, spotted Nellie in all her finery. He literally did a second take.

'Nell!' he gasped in amazement. 'Why, Nell!'

He walked slowly towards her, taking in the vision spread before him, and knelt down in front of her while she blushed and dimpled like a young girl.

'Aw! You looks beautiful, old gel.'

Nellie sat, enjoying every minute of it.

'There!' she said to my mother. 'I told 'ee that Jarge likes me to dress up!'

Yes, Jarge loved his Nellie, and looked at her with a young man's eyes.

'I never minds what my Nellie spends on clothes,' he smiled. 'It's worth every penny.'

Nellie and Jarge was a true love story, and he sang and played her his love songs up until the day she died, which was very sudden and merciful. I missed her, as we all did. She was big and colourful and left a huge gap in our lives. Jarge missed her greatly. Night after night he sat on the steps of his wagon, playing his accordion and still serenading his beloved Nellie.

On the opposite side of the gate, to the right-hand side, was where Uncle Tom, his wife Doreen and their two boys lived, my cousins Paul and Tony, his younger brother. They also had a wooden hut and a wagon.

Doreen was a *gadje* but looked more like a Gypsy than we did. She was dark and very attractive. Tom was my father's brother. He had a lovely nature. He called his wife 'My Doreen' and she called him 'My Tommy'.

If my mother had to go out without us, which was seldom, she would just let it be known among my aunts that she was going out, and everyone would keep their eye on us. If Doreen was cooking, she would call us in and feed us; maybe sausage and mash, or apple pie and custard. I hated my mother going out without me, but it was almost worth it to be given a plateful of Doreen's wonderful food. She looked after her family so well, and they were her life. She not only did her own chores but helped my uncle Tom when he went out with his lorry, buying and selling all sorts. She was educated enough to be able to do all their own paperwork and fill in any forms. Doreen knew full well that Paul was the bane of my life. He taunted me unmercifully at every opportunity.

'Paul's going to marry you one day, Rosie!' she would tease.

'Oh, no he's not!' I would reply indignantly.

'Aah. You wait and see.'

I knew for sure that I would *never* marry Paul.

Immediately behind Tom and Doreen's hut was Granny's hut and wagon. Granny's hut was where all the family seemed to gather, and was the hub of our little community. To the side of this was Aunt Prissy's beautiful wagon wonderfully painted in reds and blues outside, and a large square tent with a wooden floor and a stove in the middle. Inside it sparkled with glass and crystal mirrors, which pulled across two double beds in a similar fashion to my parents' own wagon. The wagon was fitted throughout with everything needed for everyday living but was the best, and sparkled with colour. She had the best china, crystal glass, pure white linen and lace. There was no room for clutter. Aunt Prissy was my father's elder sister. She had four daughters, my cousins Mary, Prissy, Betty and Rosina, all very attractive girls. We knew nothing of her husband, except that he was dead.

Aunt Prissy was tall and thin with a handsome face. We sometimes sat in her tent unravelling old woollen garments so that the wool could be used to tie flowers in bunches.

'Come yer, Rosie! Do unravel this bit o' wool,' she would say. I did not mind, as it was warm and cosy in Aunt Prissy's tent.

It was on one of these cosy winter evenings that my brother Nelson leaned back against a lighted candle, setting alight his shirt. In seconds the flame shot up his back, and we all screamed in fright. My aunt Prissy beat the flames with her bare hands and in seconds they were out, leaving a scorched hole in his shirt. We did not realise then what an escape he'd had. My mother banned us from flower-making by candlelight from then on, but we still went whenever we got the chance.

Aunt Prissy suffered with kidney trouble all her life. She always did her own thing, eating very little so she kept very slim and refusing to give up her daily glass of brandy.

Sometimes she would go out with her basket, which

was very heavy, and become too poorly to get home. She would appeal to someone, male or female.

'Could yer give us a lift 'ome, mister?'

She would arrive home in some kind soul's posh car and, thanking them kindly, would offer them a three-penny piece or even a sixpence. I do not know what they must have thought of this, but Aunt Prissy explained her actions to Mum.

'They can afford a car, so they don't need my bit o' money!'

She loved smart clothes, and always looked very nice whenever she went out. One day she came home in a beautiful brown coat. My mother told me later it was made from wool and cashmere and cost forty pounds. Our Granny had scolded her for spending so much money, but Aunt Prissy didn't mind, and swanned about in her new coat, which she knew suited her very well.

She also had some pretty rings, and one day we were jumping over the ditch which led from the wash-house drain when I saw a glint in the soapy water trickling down the gully. Very carefully, I grasped the treasure in my fingers and realised it was a gold ring with blue stones. I placed it on my skinny finger and paraded around with my hand held high, then ran to show my mother my prize. Her mouth fell open in shock.

'Where did you find this? It's Aunt Prissy's ring!' she gasped as she snatched it from my finger. Then she rushed over to Aunt Prissy to return it, telling her where I had found it. She gave me three pence, and I was as pleased with that as she was to get her ring back.

Of course, with so many aunts and uncles there were lots of newly married couples and, in turn, lots of new babies. To us children, it seemed like they would just appear suddenly. We would line up, waiting our turn to see this new and perfect being. We took it for granted that the doctor brought the babies in his doctor's bag, and thought this a very sensible way of doing things. All the babies were loved and made welcome. The fact was that another baby meant that everything had to be stretched still further. Somehow we managed, as any other family managed during those hard years.

Many of our aunts named their newborn infants after another member of the family. This could have caused confusion as, for instance, my name was similar to my cousin Rosina. So in order not to mix us up, everyone called me 'Baby Rosie', and my cousin Betsy was called 'Baby Bet'. This was all right if you *were* a baby, but not if you were five or six or, worse still, older. But the names stuck, and we continued to answer to these baby names until the custom finally petered out.

Aunt Amy and Uncle Fred Bailey had three sons and four daughters. Young Freddy, Bobby and Henry and Young Amy, Betsy, Valerie and Carol. They all helped Uncle Fred with his animals, and cutting and selling logs. Young Amy, being the eldest girl, helped her mother look after the youngest who were still at school. Uncle Fred had eventually built a cabin-style home on the bit of land they called home, and Aunt Amy made it into a comfortable home for them all.

Uncle Fred used to load up his logs onto his lorry in

the morning about the same time as Uncle Leonard did, both being in the same line of business.

'Can I help you today, Uncle Fred?' I asked one day. He was a lovely man with a gentle nature. He certainly did not need my help when he had all his children around him, but he kindly said, 'Yes.'

Picking up the nearest log in the pile, I threw it as hard as I could onto the lorry, or so I thought. I do not know how it happened but to my horror, it clunked Uncle Fred on the side of his head.

'Sorry! I didn't mean to do that, Uncle Fred!'

'No matter,' he groaned, rubbing his head.

I did exactly the same thing the next time. Uncle Fred watched me pick up a third log.

'It's all right, Rosie, I think we'll be able to load the rest on our own.'

I cannot believe how kind he was. If that had been my father, he would not have let me have a second go. I suppose that with seven children, Uncle Fred had learned to be patient. He used to call us to come and see all the baby animals when they were born: piglets, lambs, foals and donkeys. He worked hard, but always made it look like fun.

Aunt Amy used to go out with her basket, selling all sorts of useful things at people's doors or in Weston Town on a Saturday. She would stand on the corner of Meadow Street and Orchard Street with her basket of flowers and decorative items, and was a well-known character in the town for many years. She usually wore a very bright scarf, loosely tied around her neck, and a pretty felt hat trimmed with flowers. She also wore gold hoop earrings, gold sovereigns on chains and gold rings on her fingers, as do many Romanies. She also 'told fortunes', and had many women clients and was in great demand.

Having such a large family, she always had huge amounts of washing which she did in the late evening ready to put on the line the next morning. Her long washing line stretched right down to the paddock and was full of shirts and sheets, snowy white and blowing in the wind.

'There!' she would say proudly, hands on hips. 'Look at that washin'! Ain't it lovely?'

She usually sang while she worked, and had a very powerful voice. The summer evenings would resound with her songs. Her favourite was 'Felix Kept on Walking', and she would sing this over and over far into the night. I liked the song, but my mother used to mutter a bit.

Aunt Amy would only smoke at Christmas. She would have her hair permed, put on her best clothes and walk around looking very pleased with herself. My mother liked Aunt Amy a lot, but when she did this she would say, 'Amy's a happy woman. All her ducks are swans.' I used to wonder what she meant then.

My Aunt Brit (short for Britannia) was younger than Amy. I really loved her, as she was always very kind to us children. On summer Sunday mornings I would wake early and listen as Aunt Brit sang out the old songs in her clear voice as she made herself busy lighting the camp fire and putting the large black kettle on to boil. There it hung on the kettle iron in the very centre of the red-hot fire. Soon it would boil and as it was always very full, the water would start to spit out of the spout, hissing and sending out clouds of steam. Carefully, Aunt Brit would heave it off the fire and place several spoonfuls of tea in the old brown enamel teapot and would make the tea. When she poured it out it was a rich dark brown, but with a few teaspoons of sugar it was delicious.

As young as she was, Auntie Brit was like a mum to us. She had time to play, time to talk and time to put a plaster on a grazed knee or kiss it better. She was calm and kind and exuded gentleness and love. To look at she was small and a little plump with long light-brown hair, smiling brown eyes, beautiful skin and perfect white teeth, which she still possessed when she died at the age of eighty-six.

She would spend whole afternoons with us children picking cowslips, primroses and blackberries for a little money to buy a new blouse or a pair of shoes. She usually had a few sweets in her pinny pocket to give to a child who was feeling a bit off colour.

On Sunday mornings there was a cowboy serial on the radio called *Riders of the Range*. I loved it, and Aunt Brit always let me listen to it on Granny's radio. I never missed it if I could help it, but often the battery was so flat that I had to sit with my ear pressed against the speaker to hear it. Granny was the only one to own a 'wireless' in the camp. It was a luxury to us; money was needed for other things. When I was very young, I used to think that people lived inside the box.

I used to have to go and get the wireless battery

charged, and my cousin Rosina would come with me. An old man and his wife used to do this in their garden shed in the village. They charged sixpence for the service, which was quite a lot then, so sometimes there would be no radio for days until sixpence could be scraped together. Rosina would always carry the battery there and I would carry it back, often splashing my legs with battery acid, resulting in burns on my legs. It was a sacrifice worth making, I thought, for a chance to spend half an hour with closed eyes, being transported to the land of the free and a world of dashing young cowboys who galloped about in the hot sun, rounding up the cattle and protecting the homestead.

The thing I loved most about my extended family was the fun everyone got out of life. Yes, there were quarrels and fallings-out from time to time, but grudges were never held and anger was soon forgotten. It had to be. We lived in such close proximity, we could not have survived if quarrels had kept going. Any excuse for a party or a sing-song was seized upon, though. Many nights I lay awake, listening to my young aunts and uncles taking it in turns to sing or perform a jig. I fell asleep to jokes and laughter, and often woke to singing as well, as my aunts went about their jobs for the day. No wonder I often dream about my childhood, and long to be back there again. In retrospect, it seems like paradise.

Granny and Granfer would sit in front of the old range every evening, hardly exchanging a word, yet always content in each other's company. We children would loll about on the horsehair sofa, laughing, chatting and absent-mindedly pulling stray horsehair from our seat. In the autumn we were allowed to roast chestnuts on an old shovel pushed into the red-hot cinders. Now and again Granny would tell us to be quiet, and we were, for five minutes.

Even cleaning Granny's knives and forks could be turned into an occasion to have fun. We would sit with an old newspaper on the table, fetch the scouring powder and metal polish and off we would go, telling jokes that we had told many times before, yet still finding them funny.

'You'm s'posed t' be cleanin' they knives an' forks, you gels,' Granny would say, 'not waggin' yer tongues. Yer must 'ave a 'inge in the middle. Yer never bides quiet.'

'We don't need to keep quiet, Granny! We be usin' our 'ands, not our tongues!' Violet laughed. Of course, we both found this remark highly amusing, and laughed more than ever. Even Granny had to smile.

'Mary Ann, 'ee got to be up early in the mornin' to catch these chavvies out!' Granfer would say.

Granny tried to look fierce, but said no more. Sometimes one or two of my older cousins would join in. We played word games, like I Spy. This would have been all right if all of us knew how to spell, but as this was not the case, the game often ended in a shambles.

Granny and Granfer had one pair of glasses, which they shared. Granny would decide to do a bit of sewing.

'Edwin!' she would suddenly say. 'Lend me thy glasses – I need to threadle my needle.'

Sometimes he would reply, 'I'll threadle it for 'ee, Mary Ann.'

So he would struggle for several minutes and then remove the glasses in order to see better, and the needle was 'threadled' in seconds. He would swing around triumphantly, and we all had a bad case of hysterics.

I don't remember the exact day Aunt Prissy died, but I well remember how her eldest daughter, also named Prissy (shortened from Priscilla), cried, heartbroken, for days. Her heart-rending sobs could be heard echoing around the camp. As a child I found it a frightening and terrible sound, never having experienced grief before. Everyone tried to console her in their own way, but nothing cold stop the uncontrollable wailing. Finally, the doctor had to be called and she was given a sedative. She fell into a deep sleep on Granny's old horsehair sofa, sleeping all that day and night right through until morning. When she came to, she looked perplexed.

'Why am I 'ere on the sofa?'

'Because yer mother's died,' Granny stated bluntly.

It was just as if Prissy had heard the sad news of her mother's death for the very first time, and immediately burst into heaving sobs yet again. She did calm down a bit, but her distress unnerved us all.

As children, we were told nothing of the funeral arrangements, which were discussed in hushed tones by the adults. The next thing we knew, hundreds of wreaths and flowers arrived in an endless stream, scenting the air all around the camp. The children, not realising what all this meant, crowded around, admiring the colourful display. All we knew of the funeral was that everyone dressed in dark clothes, and they and the flowers disappeared into big black cars. Aunt Prissy was buried in the smart brown coat she was so proud of.

Later when they returned home there was a lot of whispering, and more tears from Prissy's four daughters and some of my aunts. My mother looked terribly sad and very pale.

'Can't you put a stop to this, Eddy? It's not right. What about Prissy's girls?'

I knew then that something was going on that I didn't understand. My father looked adamant.

''Ee don't understand,' he sighed. 'It's got to be done. It's the old ways.'

My mother said no more and turned away. She looked angry, but I didn't like to ask why. I found out as soon as it got dark. We were taken along to stand before Aunt Prissy's beautiful *vardoe*. There was complete silence. Suddenly a flame shot out of the roof of the *vardoe* and we all watched as it licked hungrily at the brightly coloured paintwork. Very quickly it was completely ablaze, and we all stood well back and gasped as smoke and sparks spat out into the night sky. The flames leaped higher and higher, lighting up the faces of all present. All the women and most of the children wept and moaned, and their cries and the crackling flames got louder as the wagon burned. I clutched my mother's hand, and as I looked up I saw tears in her eyes.

'That was the girls' home,' she whispered. That was the only prayer uttered that sad night.

Schooldays

I started school at four and a half, as did most children. Before going, I wondered what school actually was. My big cousins went there, I knew that much. My own little world was so full of other interests that I had hardly tried to imagine what it would be like. When I did, in my childish way, I imagined it to be like a huge Noah's Ark with sloping floors like a rowing boat. Therefore, when my mother took me on the first day, I was amazed to see that the floors were quite flat. As I had never been inside any building or even a private house before, I had nothing to go by. The teacher must have thought me very stupid, as I was so busy coming to terms with this reality that I didn't speak a word for several days.

I remember the noise and confusion when we first entered the class, and then the utter silence in which we had to sit for the rest of the day, which was totally baffling. I was used to singing to myself as I went about my childish business. No one had ever told me not to. Now I received a sharp rap across my knuckles every time I started to sing. My hands would be quite sore at the end of the day, but I found it very hard to do my schoolwork without accompanying myself in song.

The infants' class was very small, about twelve or fourteen feet long and about the same wide. The windows were tall and too high to look out of, so we would not be distracted by passers-by. Heavy, black, dusty blackout curtains hung on either side, and jam jars filled with wild flowers in various stages of decay lined the window sills. It was the girls' job to empty these each day and refill them with fresh water, but often this was forgotten so the room reeked of stagnant water. This, added to the rubbery smell of plimsolls and unwashed bodies, made an unforgettable odour that meant you had to hold your breath for as long as possible when entering the room until you became acclimatised to it.

My mother took me in on the first day and I felt completely abandoned as she walked to the door and gave me a little wave before disappearing. I immediately ran to the door, frantically trying to open it, but it would not move.

'Mammy! Mammy!' I screamed.

The teacher caught me by the arm.

'Behave yourself, Rosemary!' she said, harshly. 'Behave yourself, or you will stand in the corner!'

At first, I did not realise that she was speaking to me because she called me 'Rosemary', and I had always been called 'Rosie' or 'Baby Rosie' at home, so I took no notice of her. Grasping me by the shoulders, she pushed me across the room until I stood facing the wall in the corner of the room.

'Stay there. When you can behave, you may join the rest of the children.'

I was very frightened, as I did not know what was happening, so I turned around to look at what was going on behind me.

'Turn around and face the wall!' she shouted.

I jumped, and then I wet my knickers. The teacher, who I discovered later was called Miss Farr, sent me out to the cloakroom and found me a pair of clean knickers that had obviously been kept for the purpose. When I returned, she spoke to me very kindly. She must have realised how strange everything was to me, and she was very gentle with me for the rest of the day. When I finally went home, I was surprised to learn that I would be going again the next day and for lots more days, for years to come.

Around the schoolroom was a beautiful wooden frieze consisting of hand-painted letters of the alphabet with a picture next to each letter. I really loved it, and although I already knew my ABCs because my mother had already taught me to read, I would gaze at it for ages. We were also given trays of sand and shells to play with, which I thought very strange and utterly boring. After all, there were only a few things that you could do with a tray of sand. The slates we were given made a horrible noise when we used the special pencil. It really did set our teeth on edge. The classroom was never warm enough for small children. Sometimes we were allowed to wear our coats in class, but our coats were usually hand-me-downs from older members of the family, so they did not keep out the cold much, as they were so worn out. When we came to school wet through, our coats had to be put on the radiators to dry out and this made the room colder still.

Miss Farr and the other teachers had a cup of tea mid-morning and she used to toast a slice of bread in front of the fire. This took ages, but the wonderful smell of toast pervaded the classroom and most of us were drooling by the time it was ready. Miss Farr would cut the slice into small cubes and choose a child from the front row and give him or her a morsel. I thought this a very strange thing to do. Most of the class had come to school with no food inside them at all and could have eaten half a loaf, much less a small cube. However, the child that was given the toast always looked very pleased to be chosen.

My cousin Johnny was chosen one morning. Johnny was very well fed and was quite a round little boy. Miss Farr offered him the morsel on the end of a fork. Johnny looked at it scornfully.

'I don't want yer dry bread, Miss. I've already 'ad three slices of toast an' butter fer me breakfast! Give it to the birds, Miss.'

'Don't be rude, John!' Miss Farr's face reddened.

Johnny did not know what she meant. He did not think he was being rude, just telling the truth. Johnny's father worked hard, night and day, and the family always had enough to eat. If any of us happened to be playing with Johnny over at his place, we were always fed as well. A small piece of dry toast did not impress him at all. I did not notice her offering her toast around after that.

Johnny hated school, and went as little as possible. He used to do all sorts of things to annoy his teacher, his favourite being the sudden whistle. When the class was quietly working, or having a story, he would suddenly emit a piercing whistle. By the time the teacher had recovered her senses, Johnny would be sitting there, the picture of innocence.

'Was that you, John?' she would enquire, suspiciously.

'No, Miss, I can't whistle, Miss,' says he, pursing his lips and puffing manfully. She knew it was him, but she could never catch him. Mark, his brother, was a really handsome little boy with curly hair, huge brown eyes and creamy skin. He had a stammer, thought to have been caused by a childhood illness. He also had a vocabulary like a Billingsgate porter.

One day, the infants teacher stroked his curls and told him how sweet he was. He pulled away from her in distaste, and gave her a steely glare.

'T-t-t-t-tilly ol' t-t-t-t-tow,' he stammered.

'What did he say, dear?' she asked, smilingly unaware.

'I don't know, Miss,' I lied. I couldn't tell her that this cherubic child she was caressing was calling her a 'silly old cow', could I?

Miss Farr was an enormously fat lady. She always wore a black dress and pearls and had several chins that wobbled when she laughed. She was very kind to me, but I only realised many years later how little she understood children. I was the only new child in her class that term, and so I had to take my turn last out of thirty or so children, to choose which toy I would like to play with most. As the toys were only played with three times a week, it was ten weeks before I could make my choice. This was an entire lifetime for a child of less than five years of age. I had ached to play with a beautiful baby doll with a china head and dressed in the prettiest red dress I had ever seen. I had never seen a doll like it, and I wanted it so much. By the time it was my turn to choose, I no longer wanted it. I didn't even want to touch it. I was indifferent to its china charms and never played with it all the time I was in that class. The lesson I learned from it is this: if it is in your power to give something, give it now. That is when gifts are really appreciated.

I had been going to school for some days, and was just getting to know the *gadje* ways of some of the children. Most of them were fairly poor and spoke to me quite pleasantly, but one or two of the girls were spiteful and called me names. I was used to the rough and tumble and name-calling of my brothers and cousins, but it was never in a cruel and spiteful way. In fact, we were very protective of each other, and I had always been treated kindly by my family. To be spoken to in this abusive way by strangers was a real shock to me.

I stood outside the school gates, my ears ringing from a resounding slap I had just received from a fat little blonde girl.

'Gypsy! Gypsy! Dirty Gypsy!' she screamed, as the other children surrounded me and took up the cry, their faces screwed up with malice. I stood trembling, utterly bewildered, as I knew I wasn't dirty. Some of the screaming children were far dirtier than I was. I was neatly dressed, my hair in two long plaits tied with ribbons. I was certainly as well dressed as they were, yet still they screamed, 'Gypsy! Dirty Gypsy!'

Just then, two smartly dressed women approached the frantic crowd. My eyes pleaded with them to rescue me from my desperate situation. Surely they would help me. Instead, they glanced knowingly to each other and one said, 'Oh, it's only Gypsies,' as they passed me by.

At that moment, for the first time in my short life I felt exactly as those screaming children wanted me to feel: dirty and degraded. But they hadn't done it. It was the ignorance of the two people who should have been able to find some compassion for a small child in distress.

Salvation came in the shape of a red and silver cart pulled by a proud grey horse and there, on the seat, snapping his whip, was my beloved Granfer. He was dressed in his best black coat with his silver hair combed and his kiss curl neatly arranged in the centre of his forehead. Billy Pony's tail was brightly plaited with red, white and blue ribbons, and his harness and brass gleamed in the summer sun. What a joyous sight for a tired and frightened child! Granfer stopped by the gate as the silent children now stood well back. Billy Pony tossed his head once or twice and then looked straight ahead, awaiting further orders. Granfer stretched his hand towards me as though the other children didn't exist.

'Jump up, my pretty,' he said. I obeyed, watched silently by several pairs of hostile eyes.

'Gee up, Billy!' cried Granfer, cracking his whip. Exhausted, I leaned my forehead against the front board of the cart, breathing in the hot dry woody smell of the cart and the horse which blended with the safe, comforting smell of Granfer's coat – whisky and cough drops – as the sun warmed my back. He offered me a cough drop, which I slowly sucked, and rumpled my hair with his old, rough hand. He didn't say anything all the way home. He didn't have to. He was king of all he surveyed, and I was as good as anyone.

I didn't know what prejudice was until I went to school. I had always felt cared for and loved by everyone in our tight circle of relatives. I knew some *gadje* folk, but they knew us as well, and were friends of Aunt Amy's Bet and Bobby, so I always felt comfortable with them. When I went to school, however, my little world fell apart. My older cousins, Rosina, Betsy and Mary, had all gone to the village school, but whatever miseries they had encountered there they kept to themselves. They guessed that if they had come home with tales from school, Granny would have gone down the next day, probably in the middle of Bible class, and raised the roof. That would only have made matters much worse. So they fought their own battles, and when they came home from school scratched and bleeding, no one asked why. The lives that our parents lived were so busy, they had little time to worry; besides, they probably assumed that the teachers would have sorted any problems out. They firmly believed that those in authority were trained to do their job well and would be fair.

Nothing could have been further from the truth. If we ever had problems with the other children, we learned not to complain to the teachers. Most of the time they did not even listen but would stand and look over our heads into the distance. We learned never to keep any small treasures in our coat pockets, as they would surely be gone by home time. We never bothered to say anything, though; we did not see the point. However, it was quite another story when other children complained about us. Many an irate parent came down to the school about 'the Gypsy kids'. Half the time we had no idea what they were talking about.

One strange thing happened quite a few times at school. We often went to the cloakroom to get our lunch, only to find it gone. We always left our packed lunches in the cloakroom with any other bits and pieces we had taken to school. We weren't supposed to take anything of value but of course, we all did. Some of the children may have called us 'dirty Gyppoes', but that did not stop them from stealing our lunch. Quite a few of the *gadje* children were from poor families and could not afford three meals a day, so they would ask to go to the toilet and sneak into the cloakroom, taking anything they could find. I am sure some of the teachers must have known about this, but it was probably easier to turn a blind eye.

My mother made us packed lunches with anything edible she could lay her hands on. We had chopped apple with a small amount of grated cheese over the top, chopped dates, grated carrots and all sorts of nice things packed thinly inside sliced bread. Even the teachers were impressed, and often asked us what was in our sandwiches today. They even said my mum was clever, a rare compliment that I happily relayed to her. The only trouble with this was, mine and my brother's lunch was regularly stolen, and we went all day without food. We did tell Mum about it and she was not at all pleased.

'I'm not giving our food away to *gadjes*! We haven't got enough to feed ourselves!'

After giving it a lot of thought, she decided that she would walk to the school each day, rain or shine, and bring our sandwiches to us herself. It was a strain on our mother to do this, but we were very glad. Soon after, we heard that we were to have hot school lunches! This sounded and smelled a lot better than it tasted. School dinners gave me an everlasting hatred of many foods, unfortunately. There was nothing wrong with the food itself, but it was so badly cooked that it was rendered almost inedible. Meals cost about two shillings and sixpence per child, and Mum often found it impossible to find the money for three (soon to be four) children.

Later, when Chris came to school, it was ten shillings a week for us all. It may as well have been ten pounds. Sometimes it was the middle of the week before she managed to scrape it together. When we told her we hated the food and rarely ate it, she was relieved beyond measure and so we were back to having Mum's lovely sandwiches again. It seemed strange to think that *gadje* children did not mind eating 'dirty Gypsy' food and I do not really know why, but we would never have eaten theirs in a million years!

It is a shame that some children's lives are marred by bullying, when they should be enjoying the happiest times of their lives. Very few weeks passed in my first months of school when I didn't walk out at least twice a week and make my own way home. I was five, and it was a two-mile walk, but traffic was rare at that time and I felt quite safe.

I especially remember one of my teachers with deep affection and respect. She was a warm, kind and caring human being, and I missed her greatly when she left after just a few terms. She was the only one at the school who showed me true warmth, and was everything a good teacher should be. Dear Miss Gunning, she came into my life so briefly and had so profound an effect on me. I have never forgotten her. She arrived at our school just after Christmas. I felt drawn to her at once. She was endlessly patient and kind, and even when I went home she never mentioned it. But she did cure me.

One morning we had a spelling lesson. On the board she wrote the word HOMESICK. She looked directly at me and spoke.

'Now, Rosemary, you know what this word means, don't you?' I blushed in acknowledgement, but from that day on, I never walked out of school without a very good reason.

It was Miss Gunning who helped me make my first soft toy, a golliwog. She even found me a piece of astrakhan fur for his hair. I had very few toys, and I treasured him for years.

One day an announcement was made that there was to be a competition to see who could collect the most money for a charity. The school hall buzzed with excited whispers, but I knew I wouldn't win.

I tried hard, however, and managed to collect seven shillings and sixpence. I thought it quite a lot, but again knew I would be beaten. I handed it in and thought no more about it. The day arrived for the announcement of the winner. I gaped as my name was read out, as the winner of a lovely book entitled *Uncle Mac's Children's Story Book*. The whole school was informed that I had collected the most money – almost a pound! I was dumb-founded, as I knew it wasn't my doing, but as I glanced towards Miss Gunning with questioning eyes, she put her finger to her lips briefly and smiled. Later she told me that she had put her own money towards it and that I must say nothing. I was so happy that day.

Only one child tried to spoil it for me. She walked past me and sneered, 'What a pity you won the book. Someone like you wouldn't appreciate it.' How wrong she was! If she only knew what a joy reading was to me then, and still is. But Miss Gunning knew. Some may regard it as cheating, but others may think of it as positive discrimination. As a child of five, I didn't realise what a sacrifice Miss Gunning had made in order for me to win the book, but I have blessed her for it often.

There was another occasion when the school inspector was to visit. All the teachers appeared nervous, and there was an atmosphere of reluctant anticipation in the school. Miss Gunning just told us to do our best and to try not to let her or ourselves down.

The inspector breezed in and selected children at random to read or explain some work they had done. He then addressed the whole class and asked if any of us knew the answer to a biblical question. To my own astonishment, I stood up and recited the parable of the mustard seed from beginning to end. I hadn't even known that I knew it! I sat down to rapturous applause. Afterwards, he came and sat by me and told me I was a clever girl. Miss Gunning smiled at me, proudly.

Later that day, one of the boys made me cry by calling me a 'dirty Gyppo'. Miss Gunning called me in. I couldn't stop sobbing. She wiped my tears away and suddenly knelt down and put her arms around me.

'Rosemary, don't waste your tears on such a foolish boy,' she said. 'Rosemary is who you are. Such a pretty name. I wish you were my little girl.'

How could I ever forget her? She was a real teacher. After the summer holidays, she was gone. We were never told why teachers came and went. All I know is that I missed her, and in a strange way I miss her still. I wish I could tell her how special she made me feel in the short time I knew her. She gave me a belief in myself, and showed me the value of true kindness and a generosity of spirit. She also gave me her very own Bible, because she was so proud of me reciting the parable, especially as it was a surprise to her. I kept it until it finally fell to pieces through use, but her precious gift to me will stay locked in my heart always.

Our school was typical of most village schools, small with two classrooms and one large central room with dividers that slid back to make one large assembly hall. How we ever learned anything I don't know, because we had to strain our ears to hear our teacher above the teacher next door. Sometimes, if the lesson next door was more interesting, we would listen to that one instead of our own.

The school was encircled by a stone wall surmounted by iron spikes. On entering the gates, you came into the girls' playground. To the right was a much larger boys' playground. We spent our entire schooldays sitting next to each other in class, and yet we were separated at play, which I thought very odd. The boys were very rough, though, so I suppose it was wise.

I never liked sitting next to boys in my class. I had three brothers of my own, and although I liked them well enough I did not want to be too close to more of them in class. They were always fighting, and as the teachers turned a blind eye to torn clothing and bloody noses, they behaved like little heroes. This was very irritating as anything less like a hero was hard to imagine, but I never minded Robert Browning sitting next to me. He was so calm and quiet. He was also handsome, spotlessly clean and very well dressed. Above all he was a good boy, kind and generous to a fault, always sharing his sweets and chocolate with me. The other boys teased him and would have made his school life unbearable, but Robert would not be drawn by their taunts and would not join in their fights. He saw my cousin tugging me along by my arm one day.

'Don't do that, Paul!' he begged. 'Don't be wuff with Wosie!'

84

Because he was so gentle, his life was made miserable by the other boys. I remember him well because in spite of this, he remained peaceful and gentle all his school-days.

One advantage was that being a village school, it was small enough for us to know every child. Another benefit was that during the summer we were allowed to sit in the playground or in the school garden for some of our lessons, and we liked this best of all. The older boys did not seem to spend much time in class. We would see them walking down the road with rakes, spades and hoes. They were expected to help on the farms to take the place of the farm labourers who were in the armed forces. I do not know how good they were at farm labourers' work, but I do know that they left school with their education sadly lacking.

The school garden was looked after by the pupils, the boys digging and weeding, the girls doing the lighter work such as planting, watering and picking the fruit. In this garden, strawberries, raspberries and loganberries grew, as well as gooseberries, redcurrants and black-currants, row upon endless row. We little girls picked them for the teachers. We ate none as we were told not to, and in those days children did as they were told. Until one day, that is. One very hot day, one little girl ate a luscious red strawberry. One by one, we all stopped and watched her in amazement. Defiantly, she ate an-other, then another. Her face was already stained with juice, so we knew she would be in trouble.

'What can they do?' she shrugged. 'They've never

given us any, not even a handful, and we've picked pounds and pounds!'

One by one we started to eat the fruit and it tasted wonderfully cool and refreshing, possibly the more so because it was forbidden. After a while, some of the bigger boys came across to see what all the fuss was about and started on the raspberries, and then the other fruit was demolished. In a very short time every bush had been pillaged and not even a sour gooseberry was left. We put the ones we had already picked into a small bowl.

'Enough for a mouse's breakfast,' observed one small girl. Suddenly we realised what we had done. We had seen the pots of cream sitting on the table in the coolest classroom, and we knew we would be in *big* trouble. We stood looking at each other in dismay, the evidence staining our mouths and hands, but none of us looked sorry.

'What can they do to us, anyway? I'll bring my dad to school if he canes me!' said one boy.

'I'll bring my big brother,' said another.

One by one, we all declared who we would bring to school to sort out the teachers, but it was only bravado and we knew we would get into bigger trouble at home. We had committed a crime in brazenly stealing the teachers' fruit.

Suddenly, the garden gate clicked open and in strode the headmaster. He stopped there as though he could not believe his eyes, shaking his head and taking in the full realisation of our juice-stained faces. The empty bowls and denuded bushes told their own story. Still not believing what he was seeing, he picked up the bowl containing the few berries and shook it, as though by doing this it would suddenly become full. One of the bigger boys let out a loud snort of laughter, and we all followed suit.

Soon we were all laughing hysterically, but it was only nervous laughter. No one thought it was funny; least of all the headmaster. In fact, we were all really scared by now. He swung around and snatched a tea towel from the garden line and set about all of us, swinging it at our unruly heads. As one, we ran screaming through the gate, only to be herded into the school hall. We sat down meekly at our desks, but our class teacher merely told us to stand for the hymn and prayer. After the 'Amen', we were dismissed and filed out, glancing at each other with the same thought. Surely we would be kept in, caned or punished in some way? No, we were sent home as usual.

All that weekend I was in fear of what would happen on Monday, but nothing happened, and nothing was said outright, although we had a few remarks in assembly about stealing and being careful who you mix with, while eyes were pointedly looking at us Gypsy kids. I did not care. If the teachers had told us we could eat a few berries we probably would not have rebelled. I do know that the teachers always picked their own fruit after that.

Many of the children at the village school could neither read nor write, even after being there for some time. It seemed strange, then, that I, a Gypsy girl, could do both before I'd even started school. I knew the alphabet by the time I was three, as my mother spent a good part of her time teaching me herself. I enjoyed these lessons very much, but I had a few problems with the letter F. I could never remember it. Mum, who was usually patient, got annoyed with me and gave me a hard tap on the knee every time I forgot. I soon learned after that. My teacher at school took advantage of Mum's efforts and sent me, a five-year-old child, outside to a three-sided corrugated-iron shed to teach other children who had difficulties with reading. However, I did not mind this as I loved going outside if the weather was fine, not realising what effect it was having on my own education.

Some of the children found it easier to learn when they were away from the dreaded ruler and the bully that rapped it over their knuckles. Being a child as well as their teacher, we had fun while learning, and as I was good at making words rhyme, they soon caught on. Others would never learn, no matter how hard I tried, and mixed up their Bs and Ds or wrote them backwards. I now realise they were dyslexic. I expect there are some of them alive today who still remember those childish lessons.

School was not easy for many of us. The teachers were not fully equipped to teach us, and we were discouraged from asking too many questions. Dad was always proud of our accomplishments and praised us for them. The more I learned, the less I thought he knew, and would spend ages trying to teach him the right way about something. Sometimes he accepted it, other times he would roar like a bull at my childish audacity. Often I would worry away at him about something until he really lost his temper.

For instance, on the day I learned that coal was made from thousands of years' worth of compressed leaf compost, I could not wait to rush home to impart this wonderful knowledge to my father, who always asked me what I had learned that day. He point-blank refused to believe it, and informed me that coal was a sort of stone or rock. The more I argued, the angrier he became until in the end I made myself scarce, muttering something else I had learned that day about not casting pearls before swine. Fortunately, he did not hear me.

I feel I gained a good basic education in spite of this, and got on well in life due mainly to the inspiration I received from dear Miss Gunning. If only all the teachers had been like her! Other children, including my cousin Rosina, left school unable to read and write. However, after leaving school, she managed to teach herself to read from comics and then there was no stopping her.

As I have already said, we were not allowed to take anything of value to school, but children love to show their 'precious' things to their friends. However, Granny-in-Town took pity on me one day. It was the first time I had been to her house, and it seemed so large to me. I did not take too much notice of my surroundings, but I *did* take notice of the lunch she gave us. What a wonderful plate of jam tarts, all home made, we had for our pudding! Granny had put six on a plate, with a spoonful of cream on each. Without even thinking of others as I had been taught, I ate every one. They were tiny and could have floated away. Mum and Granny laughed and we went home with a tin full, which we shared with the family.

She took me into her bedroom and presented me with a box of necklaces and beads to play with. Emptying the pretty beads on the bed, Granny-in-Town turned on the light and the beads sprang to life, sparkling and glittering just like real diamonds. I played with them all afternoon, lost in a world of princesses, and then Granny asked me how many strings of beads I had. An involuntary tear slid down my cheek.

'None, Granny,' I answered softly, 'I haven't got any jewels.'

She put her arms around me and gave me a hug.

'You can have all of these if you like.'

I could not believe it. All these lovely things were mine to keep! When I got home, I tipped them out and chose the ones I liked the best for myself and shared the rest with my cousins. I do not know what became of the rest of those beads, but I still have a small string of the most beautiful ones. They were red, with other beautiful colours that seemed to shine through. I have been told that they are moonstones and quite valuable, but it did not matter because Granny-in-Town had made my day special. I had had a lovely day. I had been given some beautiful beads, slid down the banisters for the first time ever and was going home with the smell of newly baked pastry still in my nostrils.

The string of moonstones was at least two feet long

and even doubled up hung past my waist. I desperately wanted to wear them to school to show Miss Farr. Mum tried to dissuade me, and reminded me of the school rules on valuable items.

'They're only beads. Other girls wear pretty beads to school.'

Finally she gave in and let me wear them to school, and off I went as happy as any queen.

I proudly showed Miss Farr my lovely beads as soon as I got to school.

'Yes, they are pretty,' she conceded, 'but you can't wear them in school, you might lose them.'

She pulled me forward and instead of unfastening them she roughly pulled the beads over my head, catching them in my plaits. Dozens of tiny beads scattered everywhere. They ran all over the floor, finding every crack and crevice. Some went into the little girls' pockets. I only managed to find a few, and Miss Farr poured them into an envelope.

'You may collect them after school.'

I was so upset and wanted to keep looking, but Miss Farr said, 'No.' I had had enough. I noticed her pearl necklace sitting tightly around her fat neck and I really wanted to break *her* necklace. As if she could read my mind, she suddenly stood up.

'Go and sit down!' she demanded. 'You have caused nothing but trouble. You know you shouldn't bring anything to school. I've spent enough time on you today!'

When I got home, I gave my mother the packet of beads. She felt upset on my behalf, but she knew she could not do anything about it. She restrung the remaining beads for me, though.

Later that same week, I asked my mother to do my hair in a different style, so she plaited my hair with different coloured ribbon threaded through and pinned them on top of my head like a little coronet. I thought it looked lovely, and when I went to meet Violet for school she wanted hers done the same but there was no time.

On arriving at school, I went into my class as usual. Miss Farr called me out in front of the others and asked me who had done my hair.

'My mother did it for me,' I said, proudly.

'Well, tell her not to do it again. It's not suitable. Just plain plaits in future.'

Before I could stop her, she had pulled out my lovely coronet and left me with untidy, half-done plaits hanging over my shoulders. Bursting into tears of anger, I ran out without my coat and all the way home. Seeing me running through the yard and looking such a wreck, Mum thought I had been bullied by another child at school. When I told her what Miss Farr had done, and how she had humiliated me in front of the whole class, she went white. My mother was not one to show herself up or fly into rages, but after all the trouble I had been in, this was the last straw. Once more she combed out my hair and pinned up my coronet. Just for good measure, she pinned in a large daisy from the garden. Then she put on her best coat and shoes and combed out her pretty dark curls. With blue eyes blazing, she marched me all the way back to school.

Mum gently knocked on the classroom door.

'Come in!' called Miss Farr.

The room was quiet, but the children looked up as we entered. Mum marched in, pulling me behind her. Miss Farr quickly stood up. She had met Mum before, but Mum had always been calm and quiet, not like this steely-eyed, tight-lipped person that stood before her.

'What right have you to interfere with how I choose to dress my child?' she demanded. 'This is the second time in a week that you have ruined something of Rosemary's! How would you like to be shown up in front of the class, Miss Farr?'

'The way Rosemary was dressed and had her hair was not suitable for school,' Miss Farr replied.

'Well,' said my mother, 'I don't like *your* hair!'

To my amazement, Mum suddenly leaned forward and pulled out Miss Farr's huge hair bun. Out fell a bunch of old stockings that she was using to make the bun look bigger, and several hairpins tinkled to the floor. Some of the class started to snigger. Mum looked Miss Farr in the eye.

'I can see you love your beads, so I won't break yours as you broke my daughter's, but perhaps you might know how she felt when you broke her lovely beads and didn't even apologise!'

Miss Farr was red in the face now, and the class was silent. All her chins wobbled at once as she tried to tidy her hair.

'I'm leaving my daughter here,' Mum continued, 'but I hope she has a happier time than she had this morning!'

Mum turned on her heel and walked out.

Nothing was ever said to me again about my hair, and Miss Farr never interfered with the way I dressed.

Holidays and Happy Times

I went to that little school for more than ten years, but I don't believe I learned any more than the basics. I learned far more when I left school, and so much more from life. The best part of school, as far as I was concerned, was breaking up for the summer holidays. Standing in the school hall on the last day of term singing:

> Lord dismiss us with thy blessing,
> Once again assembled here.

This never failed to bring a tear to my eye, but joy to my heart at the thought of all the long days ahead when the world would be ours.

According to the season, we wandered the fields from morning to night, plundering the hedgerows and meadows of their free bounty of flowers and fruit, picking up wheat gleanings and rubbing them between our palms and eating the nutty kernels. We paddled in the shallow river, trying to catch the fish in our hands, but of course, we never could. Splodging in the muddy water in our old wellies, the cold water we felt through the rubber was wonderful as our feet were cool but dry.

The days were endless, but never seemed long enough for all our adventures. We revelled in our freedom, and never wanted to be anywhere else. It was harder if the weather was bad, as we were a bit short of room inside, but we were used to it. One day, however, my father said he would make us a playhouse of our very own – somewhere to play and be out of our mother's way for a bit. We watched, chattering excitedly, as he brought home an old van, pushed it into the corner of our garden and removed the wheels. In it, he put an old kitchen wood-burning stove, with its chimney up through the roof, and a couple of old chairs. We were thrilled to bits. Every cold day, we lit the fire, no one ever thinking of any danger. We were used to fires and were very careful. None of us was ever burned.

We collected pieces of coke from the clinkers that were used in the yard to keep it dry underfoot, to burn on our little stove. We spent hours in our den, some-times more than a dozen of us would be squeezed in, playing cards, 'gambling' with old pennies and half-pennies and telling jokes and stories. It was ours, but my father also kept his seed potatoes and onions in there for planting in the spring. It proved too much of a tempta-tion for us, and when Dad came to plant them, not one vegetable remained. I had gradually cooked every one in the little stove for our suppers. Baked onions and pota-toes in their jackets, with a sprinkling of salt and a knob of butter made a delicious and memorable meal. I have never forgotten those clandestine feasts. I can savour the wonderful floury potatoes and the caramel taste of baked onions even now. Dad was lost for words when he discovered his loss. He searched incredulously through the empty sacks, wondering how we had got through several hundredweight of onions between us, and feeling grateful that we were unable to eat the dried peas and beans. We got into trouble, I suppose, but I cannot remember what form it took. Knowing my father, he probably admired our ingenuity, and everyone chipped in to replace the seed vegetables.

After that, everything we cooked was legitimate. We dared not repeat the performance. We often took in bits and pieces we had begged from our mothers. Once, Dad gave us an old lantern with a piece of candle inside and it gave us a good light. Unfortunately, it scorched the ceiling, so to prevent this I found an opaque glass shade from one of the old scrap cars in the yard to shield it. It was oval-shaped and worked a treat. My brother Teddy, being used to me cooking all sorts of things on the stove, looked up in amazement at this and demanded, 'I'll tell our mam of you, Rosie, if you don't give me some of that egg!'

We laughed ourselves silly, and I still smile at the idea of him thinking I was so ingenious that I could cook an egg over a candle.

Our childhood days were overflowing with places to go and things to do. We were never bored or lonely. All our cousins living in close proximity meant we always had friends, and the world was our playground. We didn't appreciate at the time the freedom we had in such abundance, now lost and gone for ever.

Out walking with my cousin Violet one very hot summer's day, we came to a field and stopped to lean over the gate. As we gazed over the acres, we saw what appeared to be a mass of blue flowers swaying in the gentle breeze. Suddenly, as if on a signal, an enormous cloud of blue butterflies rose into the air with one accord. The air vibrated, and the sun shone on their glistening wings. We stood watching, scarcely daring to breathe. Looking down, I saw a butterfly nestling in one of my long plaits. I felt blessed, and cherished the moment. Then, with a sound like a gentle sigh, they were gone.

I well remember losing a shoe in almost the same spot. It had been raining heavily for days, so as soon as the sun shone again we were off, running wildly down the muddy lane. I was brought to an abrupt halt as my foot was sucked down into a deep muddy puddle that gripped me like a vice. Try as I might, I could not pull my foot free. With visions of being stuck there all night, I screamed in panic. Everyone came running to see what all the noise was about, and after a brief consultation on the best course of action, I was grabbed around the waist. After much heaving and puffing, I was pulled out, minus my shoe. I knew I had to retrieve it somehow. With my brothers' and cousins' help, I dug around in the mud for what seemed like hours, but we never did find it. Sucked down to who knows where, it was gone for good. I limped home in tears, an unwilling Cinderella, knowing that shoes were expensive, and now my mother would have to buy me another pair.

My father solved the problem, however, as he had been paid in kind for some work he had done for a man in the village. In the box of odds and ends was a pair of clogs – the real thing, with wooden soles. To his joy, they fitted me perfectly. They felt as heavy as lead. My life was a misery. I dragged myself through each weary day, longing for the moment when I could rid myself of those hideous clogs, and empathised with the little Dutch girl, weeping, in a picture I had once seen. I was unable to run; I could hardly walk. The only one who was happy with them was my father, who thought he would never have to buy me a pair of shoes again.

'A hop, skip and a jump and they'll be out!' he predicted direly, each time any of us had new shoes.

My mother could stand my misery no longer, and took me off to buy a new pair of brown sandals. My joy was without bounds. I ran and jumped from morning to night like the ponies in the field at the end of a working day, kicking their heels with unfettered freedom. After that, I kept well away from puddles. What became of the clogs, I neither knew nor cared.

Around the edges of the fields and in between the vegetables, we planted sweet peas from the pods we had saved from the year before. These we also sold from door to door for sixpence a bunch. I can smell the sweet peas still, remembering the happy summer evenings spent picking and bunching as we laughed and chattered endlessly. We had so much to say. We didn't have to be seen and not heard, although my uncle used to call me 'The News of the World'.

After we had finished, we would help my father pick a huge bowl of salad vegetables. We would watch him rinse off the earth under the tap in the little wooden shed, which was the only water supply for us all, and shake off the droplets in the evening sunlight. Then we would sit under the hedge with a thick slice of bread and butter and a corner of cheese, content with our own company and at peace with the world. Sometimes now, before I fall asleep, this memory comes into my mind, whole and perfect, so I can almost smell the flowers and taste the wonderful food.

To me, the sun always shone in those days. We had few toys – but who needed them? There was always someone to play with. I could pick and choose from a dozen or more cousins or young aunts. We played all sorts of wonderful games, and we never tired of making up games as we went along. Sometimes the fun would get out of hand and someone would end up with a bloody nose or have a milk tooth knocked out, but no malice was ever intended and no offence taken. I lost most of my baby teeth in this fashion because of Paul. He sometimes got annoyed with me, especially if I tried to be smarter than he was, and he would give me a quick slap in the mouth to make me mind my manners. I seemed to spend quite a lot of time spitting out my teeth, but in spite of this my permanent teeth grew very nicely, white and even. He, of course, took credit for this, saying that he had given them space to grow properly.

*

I have heard it said that it is only on looking back that you know when you were happy. I don't think this is true, as in my case I can remember moments in my childhood when I was completely and utterly happy and knew it. Golden days full of fun and laughter, every day an adventure – I can remember it as if it were yesterday – such as going for a picnic with Violet and another cousin. We each took something for the meal. I took three biscuits, one took a lettuce and the other three slices of bread and butter. We set off in the hot sun in skimpy cotton frocks and wellies. We always had to wear wellies in the fields, whatever the weather, as Aunt Betsy had a great fear of snakes and felt we were all much safer in rubber boots, as the fangs couldn't penetrate the rubber.

Little did she know that as soon as we were out of sight, we threw the wellies off under a hedge. Then we would run barefoot all the way to the river. We sat down on the grassy bank waving our bare feet in the air to cool them, and divided our repast equally, washing the lettuce in the river. I placed the biscuit and lettuce in the bread and made a sandwich that I honestly believe was the best sandwich I had ever tasted. Afterwards we had a long drink from the river. In those days we had never heard the word 'pollution'. We were always drinking river water, and remained unscathed.

Near the river was a tumbledown old cottage. In it an old man lived. We were very curious as to what he and the interior looked like, so one day, with great daring, we knocked at his door. A very bent, but polite old man answered our knock. While the others asked for a drink of water, I sneaked a look into the main room. I have never forgotten seeing that room and its contents. It was stacked almost to the ceiling with old boots and shoes in various states of decay, and the smell was almost overpowering. I heard the old man saying he always drank from the river, and there was no water in the house. As we walked away, Violet said that she was very glad, as he might have made us drink it from one of his old boots. On this hilarious note, we ran home through the twilight of a hot summer's day. The sun was going down like a huge red ball dropped in a vat of molten gold. I knew I was happy that day.

The apple tree stood in an old orchard near our camp. I loved it because although it was dying, it still blossomed profusely every year and its branches spread close to the ground, making it easy for a small child to climb. We all carved our names on its old branches, and it was a wonderful place to hide if we wanted to disappear for a while. Many a day we played there, running wild among the old trees, shouting and laughing, the sweet perfume of the blossom making our senses reel. It was almost the end of the holidays, and some of the apples had begun to ripen.

'Oi! This orchard's ours! Get out!'

Three boys from our school stood inside the gate. The tallest one had shouted the order, and he awaited our compliance with his arms across his chest. None of us was afraid of them. We knew them well, and the orchard did not belong to them.

'Dirty Gyppoes!' he snarled. The other two joined in.

'Yeah, dirty Gyppoes! Get out!'

This was war. We decided to fight back.

'Leave us alone! It ain't your orchard, either!'

Suddenly, one of them ran to the edge of the orchard and produced an air rifle. This did make us nervous, as we all knew how dangerous they were. He swaggered towards us, pointing to our tree.

'I've shot all they apples off that branch. There's only one left. I've kept that 'til last, 'cos it's the hardest one to shoot, it's so small.'

None of us believed that he had shot any of the apples down, but we watched as he took several shots at the little one. After a bit, and red-faced, he let one of his companions have a go. They had no luck either, and we were all sniggering in contempt by now.

'See if you can do any better!' he hollered, offering us the gun. No one took it.

'Scaredy-cats!' the other two jeered. Suddenly I decided I wanted to have a try.

'Let me have a go.'

They did not think I was big enough, as the gun was nearly as big as I was, but he handed it to me and stood well back. I was going to ask how far back I should stand, so I swung around, still pointing the gun. They immediately fell to the ground with their heads in their arms.

'I only wanted to know where I should stand,' I said. The three boys stood up and backed away.

'Just get on with it!'

I turned towards the tree and pointed the gun in the

general direction of the apple and fired. Nothing happened for what seemed like ages, but as we watched, the apple slowly dropped to the grass beneath. No one was more surprised than me, and I gazed at the empty branch in shock, as did everyone else. The village boys silently took the gun and walked away to our hoots and jeers.

I realise now that somehow the apple stalk must have been weakened by being shot at, so that when I shot it, it must have been the last straw so to speak. However, the boys did not know that, so they left us in peace rather than be shown up again.

We continued to play in our apple orchard playground, not needing swings or climbing frames. We used our imaginations, and became everything from cowboys and Indians and slightly scruffy princesses in the tower. It was easy enough to let down our hair as it was very long, and this was fine as long as the boys kept to the rules and did not tie our long tresses to a branch only to run off and leave us there. Give us a few trees, a trickling stream and a patch of grass, and we were happy all day long.

Down by the broken fence was a little pond, which we had made bigger over the years. Behind it stood an apple tree, which blossomed abundantly every summer. In the autumn it bore the biggest plump green apples I ever saw. They looked as though they would taste 'most beautiful', as Granny would say. They actually tasted of nothing. The flesh was soft and watery like an old turnip. Somehow we could not believe that these lovely-looking apples 'tasted of nowt'. The disappointment was intense. Every year we tasted the apples, hoping that by some miracle they would taste as apples should taste.

'It must've growed from an apple core,' said Granny as she spat her mouthful into the bushes. 'Nobuddy with any sense would plant a tree with apples that tasted of nowt!' Granfer agreed.

'It's growin' under false pretences!'

My mother was the most disappointed of all of us. She tried cooking them all different ways but they were still tasteless. The tree itself did give us many laughs over the years. Passing village children scrumped the fruit and even cars stopped and the occupants helped themselves to those beauties. We imagined their faces when they discovered that even an old turnip would taste better.

However, the tree smelled wonderful when it was in blossom, and gave shelter to us and our small pond on a hot sunny day. All of us little girls would sit at the edge and look for frogs and frogspawn. We hoped that one day the spawn would turn into tiny fish instead, but of course that never happened. We enjoyed playing with the baby frogs, and always returned the escapees to the pond. Sometimes we would make little shelters out of an old blanket draped across the lower branches, and play mammies and daddies like any other girls.

The river was our playground, and we spent many happy hours in summer playing in the water, although none of us could swim. We had great respect for the river, though, as we had been told over and over again of the dangers. I had never heard of a drowning, and we had all fallen in at some point, but we never came to any real harm, just a good wetting now and then. A family lived just down the road in the village, and the two younger boys used to join in the fun as they were friends with my cousin Bobby.

They had built what they called a 'raft', and we spent most of the school holidays playing on it. We had a long pole we had dragged there from the scrap yard, and we used this in punt-like fashion up and down the quietest part of the river. Sometimes the pole got stuck in the mud and whoever was 'punting' would be left floundering.

Catching perch, or trying to, was a favourite pastime. There seemed to be shoals of these fish, but we never were able to catch any. We would lie for ages on our bellies scooping with jam jars held by bits of string, but the little fish seemed to know what we were up to and bypassed our traps. After a while, we would get bored of this.

'Come on,' someone would shout, 'let's see who can climb the old oak!'

We would whoop and scamper up to the challenge, sometimes giving in and sitting under its shady boughs. The boys were good at it, and went home with bloodied knees from the tree bark. We did not waste our time when we were out, and regularly took home mushrooms, crab apples and blackberries. We loved summertime, and would all get as brown as berries.

My cousins, brothers and I loved to play in a place we called 'The Grassy Lane'. A small river ran along one side, and thick bramble bushes grew on the other. It had a gate at either end, and it was carpeted with lush grass and meadow flowers. There were never any animals in this small piece of pasture land, so we could more or less do as we pleased. I never minded cows, but one or two of the others did not like them and gave them a wide berth.

It was hot, and we thought we would go there and play in the cool grass. At one end the bank sloped down into the water, which was crystal clear. A little duck-weed drifted across the surface and the sun sparkled on the water and shone into my eyes, making me close them for a second or two. We were young, and could not fully appreciate how fortunate we were to be in that lovely place. Strangely, we did not go there often. It was almost as though we were keeping it for 'best', or for a special occasion.

We took off our sandals and paddled in the water, which was almost warm. The boys walked further down the riverbank and we heard the splash as they jumped in. We took no notice. We were too busy with our own affairs. After a while, we moved across to the hedge and began picking blackberries, chattering and eating as many berries as we put in our baskets. A large, sun-warmed blackberry tasted delicious. Then we started to pick bunches of the wild flowers and grasses.

'Look, I've found some shaky grass!' exclaimed Violet. It had a tall stiff stem and its little branches had tiny heart-shaped seeds hanging from them. We called them 'shaky grass'. I do not know if that was the real name, but the name we gave it described it perfectly as the seeds would continually shake in the breeze. I have not seen it for years, and I wonder if it still grows in the grassy lane. We had a magical day there, until suddenly we heard a low moan. We had not noticed that the bottom gate was open.

As we looked up we saw thirty or forty cows making their way in through the gate. We were not really worried until we realised that they were not cows but steers, and this did make us nervous. As long as we kept calm and walked away carefully everything would be all right. One of the young ones started to cry. The steers lifted their heads and listened. The crying child started to run back up the slope.

'Don't run!' we cried. But then everyone panicked and started to run. It was a silly thing to do, as we knew they would give chase. Sure enough, they did. It was like a mini-stampede. Instead of staying in the river, the boys got out, leaving their clothes behind. As naked as the day they were born, they ran like the wind. I suddenly realised that we would never reach the top gate in time. Taking my courage in both hands, I crashed through a gap in the bramble bush and the rest followed suit, except for my cousin Johnny and one of the other boys. They turned around and, clapping their hands, shouted at the steers as loud as possible. The steers stopped running and began to crop the grass. We could not believe that we had been so foolish as to run when we all knew better.

I started to walk home with the girls. The boys realised that their clothes were a long way down the riverbank, and they could not walk home naked, so they walked back slowly, watching the steers warily. The animals ignored them and went on cropping the grass.

We had to explain our scratches to our parents, and

they scolded us for running when we knew not to. The scratches took a while to heal, but I wrote an essay about our escapade and got ten out of ten, so I suppose some good came out of it.

If I had one wish, it would be that all children could have the unending freedom that we had. The hours we spent in the fields picking flowers to sell on the streets or door to door. I remember picking cowslips with my aunt Mary. She was my father's youngest sister, and my father adored her. She was very pretty with a small pointed chin and nut-brown curls. Sometimes I went with her to collect moorhens' eggs, as Granny liked them. Aunt Mary always knew if the eggs had babies inside them. She could pick up an egg, then replace it in the nest.

'We can't take these,' she would say. 'There's chicks inside.'

I used to ask myself, how does she know? I don't know why I did not ask her as she would certainly have told me. One day I did a wicked thing that has stayed with me until this day. After Mary replaced one of the eggs in the nest and walked on a little way, I picked up the egg, turning it this way and that. I could not work it out. How could she tell? Without thinking about it, I dropped the egg on a stone. It smashed open and sure enough, there was a baby chick inside. Mary turned and saw what I had done. She was usually a quiet girl, but now she was very angry with me.

'That was a wicked thing to do, Rosie,' was all she said.

I certainly felt wicked, thinking about the baby bird

that would never be hatched. That was the first and last time I ever harmed a helpless creature. She hardly spoke to me for the rest of the day, but as we neared the dairy that sold all kinds of nice foods including ice cream, she went in and bought two, one for her and one for me. I felt a little better and she never mentioned the matter again, but I never forgot, and in the end it taught me a hard lesson.

Mary knew where all the different types of flowers grew. There were no pesticides, and the air vibrated with the sound of bees and a million other insects.

'I'll show you where the white violets grow,' she confided one day. 'But if you shows too many people they'll soon die off.'

I told no one. I especially wanted some white violets. They were my mother's favourite, but they were very rare and this was the first time I had seen any; a large clump with masses of heavily perfumed white flowers. I just wanted to bury my nose in them. I waited a few days until I was alone, and then made my way back to the place that Mary had shown me. I picked a huge bunch, and made a beautiful posy encircled with dark green leaves. All the way home I buried my nose in the deeply perfumed blossoms. Blue or purple violets have no perfume, only white ones do. When I got home and gave them to my mother, she was so surprised. She just held them to her face, inhaling their scent. I dug up a small root and planted it in Mum's garden. It never took, but Mum always remembered those pretty white violets.

★

I found it strange that when we were taken on 'nature walks' at school – which we did enjoy, as we were out in the fresh air – we were told: 'Today, we will try and find the first celandine' (or buttercup, or whatever flower was in season). We did not seem to enjoy these nature lessons as much as the *gadje* children because nature was all around us in our everyday lives. Pretending to find a flower that we had seen growing for weeks before seemed so odd to us. So did leaving a bowl of tadpoles in the classroom before the holidays, only to return and find them turned into frogs and hopping all over the room. I thought it would have been much more sensible to put them back in their pond before we left at half-term, though it was fun catching them.

My cousin Henry was very clever with his hands and a pen knife. He would cut some branches from a withy bush and make us all whistles.

'Look, Granny and Granfer! Look what Henry's made us!' we shouted. The racket that nearly a dozen children all blowing home-made whistles created was unimaginable. Granny and Granfer put up with that for a very short time before chucking us out. Then we marched around the yard, a very strange band, blowing away until Mum made us shut up. No one seemed to blame Henry, who would slope off grinning all over his face.

As children, our days were rarely planned. If there were jobs to do, then they had to be done first. Then we did what we wanted to do. Mum never had money to waste, and any special day had to be planned down to the last penny. We went to the beach at Weston-super-Mare about twice a year, if Mum had managed to save a few coppers. We could not go more often than that as Mum had to pay for our dinners and bus fares. The four of us shared a bucket and spade, which we had for years and which caused much squabbling on the beach.

We took sandwiches and a glass bottle of orange squash, and if Mum had saved enough we might have a small ice cream cone! We all hoped the sun would shine and as far as I can remember, it always did. We had a lovely day out, gritty sandwiches, warm squash and all. The shoreline was strewn with seaweed and tiny finger-nail-shaped shells coloured pink, white and pale blue. We had to walk over yards of these to reach the sea if the tide was in, although, being Weston-super-Mare, we often had to wait for hours, watching and waiting for the sparkling waves to meet us. We came home smelling of the sand and the sea, and talked about these lovely days out for weeks because they were so rare.

However, summer was coming to an end and autumn was approaching. Were our days at the beach more exciting than playing in the river or running wild across the fields? No, just different. Each day was new and an adventure, so our day at the beach was a pleasant memory to add to all the others, and autumn would have its own reward.

As the end of summer approached and the nights began to draw in, the air had a wonderful frosty feel to it. This would signal evenings at Granny's, spent around the range. My father or uncles would bring home hazel-nuts and sweet chestnuts as a treat, and we would roast them and try and eat them too soon, burning our fingers in the process. We would sometimes have green walnuts, and they could be pickled. I was not fond of these, preferring to break them open and eat the white flesh. I thought them nicer than the ripe ones. The outer husks used to stain my fingers so badly, though, that it took weeks to get my hands clean again.

In the autumn the children would gather up the vegetation left after all the peas, beans and other vegetables had been harvested. In the middle of the field we would place a few old tyres we had begged from my father and uncles from the scrap cars, and then empty all the vegetation we had collected on top. We added any other rubbish we could find until we had a mountainous pile.

All of this took place weeks before Bonfire Night, and although we knew the story behind Guy Fawkes and the gunpowder plot, we could not reconcile our bonfire and the happy time we had with the annual burning of the effigy of a man who had tried to blow up the Houses of Parliament. We had little idea of what it all meant, but it seemed a bit too barbaric for us children.

We seldom had any fireworks, as our parents wouldn't spend money on things that only lasted a few seconds, even though they gave us all so much pleasure. On the night itself we would beg from late afternoon onwards for my father to light the bonfire. At dusk he obliged, and it didn't take long for it to start flickering. What a blaze! We couldn't get anywhere near it, the heat was so intense, and the thick, acrid smoke could be seen for miles until darkness fell.

A little while later, a few local boys who had seen the

blaze from the village arrived in the field. They knew they would be welcome as they had brought fireworks.

After setting off the bangers (which I hated), they tried to let off some sky rockets. They couldn't get them to light, and by now most of the adults had wandered back to the camp. The three boys bent over one of the rockets, blowing, prodding and poking. Suddenly, without any warning, the rocket whizzed up through the small space between their bent heads and into the night sky. I shall never forget the look of shock and terror on their faces in the glow of the bonfire, and the relief when they realised they were unhurt. We told no one of this terrifying incident, but it taught me a lesson.

We all loved the autumn evenings, but it was a bit different having to get up for school on bitterly cold mornings. We went to school often on just a cup of tea and a piece of bread. If Granfer had lit the camp fire, we would stand and toast our legs for a few minutes before leaving. The fronts of our legs would be hot and the backs frozen, but by the time we got to school we would be chilled through to the bone. The boys had to wear short trousers summer and winter, and their poor knees would be purple and raw, chafed by the cold wind. The only heating at school was behind the teacher's desk, and it never reached any of us. There were a few radiators throughout school but they only ever seemed to get lukewarm. I was never warm at school in the winter, and my lips were always chapped. I was so thankful that we were always warm at home in the evenings. Our little stove was constantly red hot, and so was Granny's.

I would read my brothers stories from my school-books at bed time, or Mum would tell us a story she had read when she was a child or a poem or two. They enjoyed the stories but were not bothered with poetry. I, on the other hand, revelled in it. I only had to hear a poem once or twice and I could remember it and recite it myself. I used to love those cosy evenings when we were all together, making toast on our little range.

On cold winter days or evenings, we were hard pressed to find anything different to pass the time. We did have a few board games like draughts and snakes and ladders, which had been given to us or bought at village sales. So we devised some games of our own. Mum had a little wooden box full of buttons. Some of them were very beautiful, and I loved going through them, making them into sets or matching up the colours. I could spend hours doing this. I gave a particularly nice set of mother-of-pearl buttons away to someone I knew. They were black and white with tiny ships and anchors on. When I told my mother, she was very angry with me.

'You shouldn't have done that without asking me first. I was going to use them on a blouse. You'll have to ask for them back.'

My face dropped.

'I can't do that! I gave them as a present!'

'I think they were quite valuable,' she grumbled, 'and you shouldn't have given away things that didn't belong to you.'

In the end she let it drop, but I never again gave away anything that was not mine to give. I had only looked upon the buttons as a plaything, and had not even considered that my mother had taken the trouble to save every one for future use and taken the time to remove them from a worn-out garment. This probably saved her a lot of money over the years.

I was never happier than when I was acting out my childhood fantasies. These were collected from the books I read. I cannot remember a time when I could not read. We used to have an odd comic or two, and maybe they would be read over and over again. By the time they fell into my eager hands, they were soft and floppy and most of the print had worn off.

'Read me a story, Rosie!' the smaller children would beg.

I would do my best to read a story from a comic, which was almost unreadable, but never mind, what I could not read, I made up as I went along. If I hesitated even for a second eager voices pleaded, 'Go on, Rosie! What 'appened next?'

I tried to oblige but it was not easy. Now and again, I was given a few pennies and was able to buy books from a jumble sale. I had borrowed a book from the school library. Most of the books there were old and donated by people who had won them for attendance at Sunday School; books like *Pilgrim's Progress* and other religious books. The children did not like the stories in them and I did not enjoy reading them.

One day my father brought home a huge box of books. He had spotted them by someone's dustbin and had asked if he could have them for me. There must have been fifty or sixty books altogether. What wealth! What treasure! The joy I got from those old books was immeasurable. Everything was there: fairy tales, religious writings and poetry, everything was grist for the mill. They opened my eyes to a world that was strange and fascinating. A world of golden-haired children, all spotlessly clean and cared for by a wonderful nanny who always gave them a daily bath and heard their childish prayers before (wonder of wonders) putting them in their own little beds for the night with their favourite toy tucked in beside them. For many years this was my dream: to go upstairs to my own bed and be tucked in by my devoted nanny, who thought me the nicest and prettiest child in the world.

One night I sat in Granny's kitchen and started reading to the other children. This book was an Enid Blyton book. As I read, my audience was listening with eyes like saucers, totally entranced. Suddenly, I was aware of the silence in the room. Not only were the children transfixed, but five or six of the adults were listening with bated breath.

'Go on, Rosie!' said Granny.

'Yes, yes, go on! Don't stop!'

'It's a good tale!'

I finished the story and then got up to go home, to everyone's dismay.

'No, don't stop readin'! That be a grand story,' smiled Granny.

After that, whenever I read a story to the little ones, any aunts, uncles or family who happened to be there listened as well. In these days of mass entertainment, it seems so strange that adults would want to listen to children's adventure tales. Most of my family could neither read nor write, and even a simple child's story made a change from the wireless.

Uncle Alfie was very tolerant of us, listening to what we had to say, sometimes joining in with his low gruff voice.

"Ee don't know 'ow lucky 'ee be to be able to go to school, learnin' to read 'n' write!' he remarked after I showed him one of my stories. I used to write short stories about cowboys and Indians, silly little tales really, but Uncle Alfie used to listen very patiently as I read them to him. He always admired what I had written, and raised his eyebrows in amazement.

"Ee never wrote that, Rosie!' he would marvel. "Ee must o' copied it!'

'No,' I replied earnestly, 'I wrote it myself!'

'Well, well. It's better than the wireless!'

Bless his heart, he used to work so hard, yet he still had time to listen and praise us. After labouring all week with my father and Freddy, all he wanted to do on the weekend was sleep on Granny's horsehair sofa. One weekend he was sleeping peacefully. Violet and I peeped in and saw him on the sofa, his head on the arm nearest the door. Giggling softly, we carefully braided his hair into dozens of tiny plaits, tying the ends with small scraps of ribbon. Alfie never stirred. After a while we went out to play, and thinking no more of Alfie's plaits, we left him to sleep. Coming back from our play later on, we were met with the sound of laughter. On seeing us arrive, my cousins called for us to come and see. When we got to Granny's out came Alfie, his hair in a riot of waves. He did not know whether to laugh or cry. Someone had loosened the plaits and his hair was left in curls.

'Bad gels! What have 'ee done to me to make me look a fool?' he growled.

We did not think he looked a fool, we thought he looked lovely. The worst of it was, a man had called to collect some tyres he had bought from Alfie and had knocked at the door, waking him suddenly. Alfie had opened the door, not realising what we had done, and could not understand why the man was looking at him strangely and trying not to laugh. Alfie had not liked to ask why, and so got rid of him as soon as possible. When he got back in, he looked in the mirror, only to see what a sketch we had made of him. Everyone in the camp came to see and thought it hilarious, except poor Alfie, of course. Although he washed it with carbolic soap, it was over a week before he got rid of his unruly curls.

When it got colder, I would collect enough coke from the clinkers in the yard that Granny had bought to prevent the yard from getting muddy, and use it to light the little stove in our playhouse. Dad warned us not to eat his potatoes so we did not dare try that trick again. We begged a couple from our mothers, and baked them and ate them with a clear conscience.

A small fair called at our village twice a year, and we young ones would beg to be allowed to go with some of the older girls. Off we would go with a few shillings clutched in our sticky fingers, most of which had been donated by our uncles and aunts.

I loved the fair. The smells of the candy floss, frying chips and hot engine oil would make our heads spin. First of all we would wander around trying to decide which ride was the best value for our money, but spent most of it on the dodgem cars. Why, I do not know because our arms would be covered in bruises by the time we went home, from being flung against the sides of the cars. The carousel we all loved. The organ music and galloping horses with their flared nostrils and flying manes went around and around in our heads long after we fell asleep. What wonderful, innocent fun it all was! Dad knew a lot of the fairground people, so we would often get free rides and toffee apples. Sometimes we would be allowed inside the caravans. These were like fairyland; spotlessly clean, sparkling crystal, Royal Crown Derby china and snow-white crocheted bed-covers bedecked these little palaces of perfection. The fairground people were so kind to us too.

When we went to school the next day and told the children and teachers how much we had enjoyed our evening at the fair, the children who had not been allowed to go were enchanted and wanted to go as well. During morning assembly, although no names were mentioned, our teacher made pointed remarks about those who had very little worldly wealth wasting what they had on rubbish at these so-called places of enjoyment, instead of spending it on the well-being of their children. It went right over our heads, so it did not worry us and it only made the other children long to go.

I was about eight when my mother and Aunt Grace swept into the playground at morning break and approached my teacher. There were a few nods between them, and then Mum came over and guided me out of the gate, and Aunt Grace collected my cousin Johnny.

'We're going to Bampton Fair, Rosie. It's too nice a day for school. What do you think?'

'Oh, yes please!' I gasped.

Johnny was as thrilled as me to have a day off school, and we jumped into the lorry with our mothers.

Bampton Fair was in Devon. It was held annually in October, and was a horse and animal fair as well as a funfair, and much larger than the little village fairs. It was a long journey in an old lorry, but well worth it. Johnny could not wait to ride the carousel, which was his favourite. He never sat still on it, though. No, he was a cowboy. While his mother was busy chatting to mine, he jumped up onto the ride.

'Gee up! C'mon, boy!' he hollered, running around the carousel and trying to mount the horses while they were still galloping up and down. I watched him in admiration as Mum and Aunt Grace looked on in not a little embarrassment.

'Whoa! Whoa, boy! This bastid 'orse won't stop, silly budder!' he growled.

My mother looked shocked.

''E's not swearin',' said Aunt Grace.

Mum was not fooled. Johnny knew exactly what he wanted to say. His hair was on end, his face red and running with sweat and his mother was frantic. He was only seven, and she thought he might fall off the ride.

'Johnny! Johnny, get off!' she screamed. Then suddenly she changed her mind. 'No! No, stay on!'

The ride finally slowed, but there was no sign of Johnny. Where *was* he? Suddenly Mum pointed. There he was on the other side of the carousel. He must have given the charge hand the slip and got back on again. The young man tried to grab him, but Johnny was like one of the eels he was always trying to catch with his mother's sieve. As the ride stopped, his mother managed to grab him by his collar. The young man tried to make Johnny's mother pay for the ride.

'What?' she spluttered. 'I should sue *you*! I nearly 'ad 'eart failure! You let 'im get on be'ind me back!'

Meanwhile, Johnny was trying to sneak back on again. This time his mother was too fast, and with the promise of an ice cream, he finally gave up.

We also went to cattle fairs and sheep fairs, where there were also a few horses or goats. Of course, these were not as much fun as the funfair, but we still loved to go. It was great to see the farmers wheeling and dealing. The animals looked so unlike their normal day-to-day selves. Spotlessly clean and brushed, they looked quite different. Dad brought home two goats after going to one of these fairs. When he brought them into the yard and my mother saw them, she clutched her head and walked away. The goats were little more than kids. One was pure white and the other black and white, and we children thought they were very sweet when they were young. They soon grew to be extremely destructive, however. They were mostly kept on a long tether, which they usually chewed through and then escaped, running through the village, striking fear and alarm into shopkeepers and shoppers alike. In the summer the proprietors would leave the shop doors wide open all day, and so the goats would run amok in the shops, sticking their noses and sharp horns into anything they could reach. The women would scream and run away, while their children flung their arms around the smelly creatures' necks and whispered lovingly into their ears. The goats would turn their faces and appear to look enquiringly into their eyes, whereupon the agitated mothers would grasp their offspring by the shirt collar and haul them out of harm's way. They would stretch their little arms imploringly towards the goats as they were dragged off.

One freezing-cold night they got loose one more time, and ran amok in Mum's garden, ruining sheets and towels. This was a disaster, as Mum had little in the way of bedding and the goats had managed to tear the lot to shreds. The washing had not dried and so had been left overnight, but the frost had made it as stiff as a board. Mum was so upset. She could not believe her eyes, and kept looking and touching the ruined washing as though she could somehow restore everything to the way it was. Granny came over to survey the damage and looked knowingly at Mum.

'Don't 'ee worry about the bedclothes. 'Ere's yer chance to get rid o' they stinkin' goats!'

Mum knew exactly what Granny meant, and patting Granny's arm, walked away from the carnage, head bowed as if in despair. Sure enough, the next day the goats were gone and no one minded a bit.

Although we didn't celebrate Christmas as others did,

we always celebrated the New Year. Everyone gathered at Granny's place. By late evening everyone but the children was a little drunk, or a lot, depending on the person. Each one would take turns in singing his or her favourite song, while all listened as quietly as they could. Any noise, and someone would shout, 'Order! Order!' at the top of his or her voice. Once order was restored, the singer would start again from the beginning. Sometimes this would go on for ages and ages, until the singer finally finished to rapturous applause, everyone comparing him or her to some famous artiste. Next, each would perform a dance or a jig to a fiddle and the spoons. This was followed by food, drink and more singing until finally my father put his 'ash faggot' on the fire. As it blazed up, everyone wished each other a Happy New Year, drank more and then went to bed. Next morning, more than a few had bad heads, so the non-drinkers had to clear up the debris from the previous night.

I remember many such get-togethers. Any excuse for a sing-song was drawn on. Everyone was welcome in our community, and anyone who called at meal times was given food or a cup of tea. Everything was shared, and many a complete stranger went away with a hot meal inside them, sometimes, as my father wryly commented, 'whether they wanted it or not!' as Granny never took no for an answer.

Travellers

*D*uring the warmer months, the travellers came to stay. These were not like the 'New Age' travellers of today. They were real Romany, but we called them travellers as that was their way of life. Some of the family names were Boswell, Loveridge and Smith. One I remember well was called 'Dirty-faced Arthur'. Why, I don't know. He always looked clean enough to me.

Down the road they came. Anything up to six or eight wagons, all brightly painted, they were a sight to see! The dogs, mainly lurchers, ran alongside the wagons and horses, the spare horses tied behind. The pots and pans in the 'kettle cupboards' at the rear rattled and clanged in time with the clopping of the horses' hooves. Small children leaned out of the windows and sat on the front seat boards, while the older ones walked alongside. There was very little traffic sixty years ago, so this was all quite safe, but of course times have changed. Granny and Granfer would make them all welcome and they stayed as long as they wanted, usually a few weeks, and then they would be on their way to the markets or the fairs. Meanwhile, it would be lovely to see new faces and have new friends to play with. A big fire would be lit and large black kettles would be hung over it, so full they would need two people to carry them. Then they would cook their meal on a big tripod over the fire, wonderful pots of stew of hare or rabbit.

In the evening we would all collect around the fire. It would look so wonderful in the dark, the flames leaping and crackling, the red glow reflecting on the travellers' handsome faces as they recounted all the gossip on people we had not heard of or seen in years. All the births, marriages and deaths were passed around by word of mouth, along with a drink of cider, and this always ended with a song and a dance or two.

One family who arrived one summer stands out clearly in my mind, simply because the mother of the family was about seven months pregnant. As she walked through the gate holding a small boy by the hand, she rested her other hand on her bulging abdomen. Her face at that moment was so beautiful, full of peace and serenity. Her skin was golden tan and her teeth white and even. Her calm, velvet brown eyes gazed around, and she moved like a queen. She was, and still is, my ideal of true beauty. All my life, no one has measured up to her. Gypsies are lovers of beauty, and really admire good looks in others. Because of this, it took me a long time to accept or befriend anyone who did not conform to my idea of good looks. It really was a mental block, and because of it my friendships were initially shallow. Luckily I found out for myself that true beauty is on the inside, and the plainest of people can have quite beautiful hearts.

*

One summer day, some travellers, strange to us, pulled in down the lane. They had a very unusual but beautiful wagon. I can still see my older cousins and aunts watching them arrive, and, linking arms, break into spontaneous song to welcome them. It sounds almost unreal when I write it down, but our lives were really like that. They stayed for a while, and Granny bought the strange wagon. We were all thrilled. I can only describe it as partly a covered wagon, and partly like our wooden caravans. Inside, at the back, there were two double beds built one above the other, the bottom bed having two doors which could be pulled across in the daytime. Two of Prissy's daughters, Mary and Rosina, used it as their bedroom for many years.

It must have been difficult to sit up under there, as there was little space and heads were often bumped. There were several small wall cupboards with glass doors, through which could be seen many lovely things that Granny had picked up on her travels, Crown Derby china and lead crystal among them. Everything in the caravan was delicate and beautifully made. Several oil lamps with porcelain bases were placed carefully on corner shelves, and on the floor were pretty hand-made rugs. On these I sat close to the little stove and listened to the tales that the girls told late into the evening. Sometimes they forgot that I was there, and I heard many secrets that perhaps I should not have!

We loved to see inside the travellers' *vardoes*. Some were a lot smaller than ours, and if they had a lot of children, the men of the family would collect withies and build small dwellings called 'benders'. They covered them with tarpaulins to make them wind- and water-proof, and then the little children would sleep in these strange bedrooms, swaddled in rugs or covered in their father's old coats. They looked snug enough in summer, but I wondered how warm they would be in the freezing winters.

In the morning, they would light their camp fires and the little ones would toddle around them. As far as I know, none was injured by these fires. The mother of each family would bustle around making big pots of tea. Breakfast would consist of fried bread for the men, sometimes fried eggs or a bit of potato. The men always had the choicest food, as they had to keep healthy and strong to look after the family. The youngest children would have bread and dripping, and the babies, bread soaked in milk. It was not much, but better than nothing and they looked well enough on it. The small boys were, without exception, very handsome with beautiful dark brown eyes, or sometimes bright blue. All had peachy skin and dark hair. Their mothers carefully combed the girls' hair into ringlets, and even the youngest children would have their ears pierced with gold earrings. They all appeared to have perfect teeth, probably because they rarely had sweets.

I sometimes wished we could go travelling, as it sounded like the best life in the world. They would sit up until late into the night around the camp fire, telling stories, laughing and singing, everyone joining in the chorus, their voices drifting towards us on the breeze. At last I would fall asleep with the echoes of their song still creeping into my dreams. It was better for us to stay in one place, though. We could go to school regularly (which was a mixed blessing), we were never moved on and we could plant and grow crops and then pick them. It was enjoyable to have the travellers visit, but it was nice to be on our own again when they had left.

If the travelling children stayed long enough, they would be allowed to attend school with us. One of them lost a valuable brooch after taking it to school. She cried, and went to see the headmaster about it. He stood looking over her head until she had finished her sorry story, and ordered her out of the room without further comment.

She was very frightened, and we were frightened for her. A small group of travellers had been camping on Granny's ground for a few weeks, and we had all got to know them well. We knew that her father was very strict and ruled them with a rod of iron. We decided to go with her while she first told her mother, who was so angry that she grabbed her long plaits and shook her relentlessly. We were not present when she told her father when he came home later, but we heard the heartbreaking screams coming from the direction of their wagon. My mother turned pale at this, and at our alarmed faces, making as much noise as she could, singing and clapping her hands, but it still was not loud enough to drown out the shouting and the child's screams. Mum gave us our supper, but for once in our lives we could not eat. In the morning, they were gone. Nothing was mentioned, at least not in front of us, and we went to school as usual. That morning the brooch turned up on the teacher's desk. Whoever had taken the brooch had thought better of it and returned it; too late for our poor little friend. The teacher simply handed the brooch to us to return to her mother. We never saw the travelling family again; why, I do not know.

One attempt at cooking an evening meal was made by a newly married Gypsy girl, and made my father laugh so much that years later he was still recounting it. The girl was still very young, about sixteen or so, and she travelled with the fairs. She was an only child, and her parents doted on her. She was also very beautiful. Her mother did all the cooking for the family, and most of the chores, while their daughter was treated like a princess.

She met her husband at one of the fairs, and it was love at first sight for both of them. Reluctantly, her parents gave their approval for an early marriage and gave them their own brand-new *vardoe*, and all their china and linen was of the very best. They did not stay with their families, but set off travelling the lanes and roads as most young Gypsy couples did in those days. For the first few weeks he cooked bits and pieces whenever they stopped along the road, or as Dad said, 'lived on love and bread and cheese'.

One day, these honeymooners stopped at Granny's gate and, as was the custom, asked if they could stay for a few days.

'O' course yer can,' Granny agreed, and opened the gate. 'Get yerselves in, and welcome!'

Their horses clopped into the yard, and all the family

came out to admire their brightly painted wagon and all their gorgeous things. Their horses were a beautiful dapple grey, and were patted and watered by the young ones, who were overjoyed to see some new faces. The first night they were welcomed by a dish of stew, sitting around the camp fire.

'Thank 'ee all,' she said gratefully, 'I'll cook 'ee all supper tomorrow night.'

'Bear in mind,' Dad recalled, 'she'd never cooked a meal in her life, nor prepared meat of any sort.'

'If the boys get lucky tonight, I'll give 'ee a rabbit,' Granny offered kindly.

'Oh, thank 'ee,' she smiled. Early the next morning Granfer took her over a big fat rabbit. Granny followed him anxiously.

''Ee'll be able to cook it, will 'ee?'

'Yes, yes, o' course,' she replied, her face whitening, and she disappeared into her wagon.

The day wore on and there was no sign of the new bride, and no smell of cooking either. The aunts exchanged worried glances but said nothing. Finally Granny could bear it no longer, and tapped on the door of the wagon. After a while, hearing nothing, she pushed the door. Tear-stained and bedraggled, the little bride was lying across the table, her hand still clutching the rabbit, and next to her on the wagon floor was a small bowl full of fur. Granny stood there silently for a few minutes, and then gently shook her awake.

'What be the matter, my dear?' she asked gently. The girl's eyes filled with tears.

131

'Oh, I'm never eatin' rabbit again!' she wailed. 'They'm too 'ard to pluck!'

At first, Granny did not know what she meant. Then light dawned.

'Haven't 'ee ever seen yer mother skin a rabbit?'

'No,' she sniffed, 'I thought 'ee 'ad to pluck 'em like a chicken.'

Her fingers were red raw. Granny gave her a quick lesson in skinning a rabbit.

'Best bake it now,' Granny suggested. 'Can 'ee finish 'im off?'

The girl nodded.

'But don't leave 'im with 'is 'ead on.'

Granny quickly chopped the head off the rabbit and left her with her prize. The girl washed the rabbit and baked it in a tin in the hot ashes. The only trouble was, as everyone discovered later from the appalling smell, she had not gutted the animal first.

'I thought 'e smelled a bit funny, but didn't know what it was,' said Granny. No one had any meat that night, just vegetable stew, which was just as well, as their appetite for rabbit had completely disappeared. The story of the young bride who tried to pluck a rabbit was remembered around the camp fires for many years.

Several years later, Dad met the bridegroom again at a horse fair. He told Dad he was very happy and had two fine sons.

'What's 'er cookin' like, then?' Dad asked wickedly.

The young man threw his head back and laughed.

''Ee thought the rabbit was bad enough – 'ee should've

seen the sprats – or what was left of 'em after she finished with 'em!'

My father just had to hear more.

'Go on, tell me,' he urged.

'Well,' the young man began, 'I told 'er once that I loved sprats, but me mother 'ated the smell, so I only ever 'as 'em once or twice. So I comes 'ome after going on the knock [begging from door to door] an' I smells fish. I 'ad a bit of a swill and she says, " 'Urry up, I've got a lovely supper fer 'ee." So I goes inside and looks at me plate. "What is it?" says I. "Sprats," says she. "It took me ages an' ages to cut off their 'eads 'n' tails an' then I gutted 'em all, but I only 'ad a small bit left, so I 'ad to go an' buy some more. But I don't mind, I knows 'ow much 'ee loves 'em!" Well, I laughed till the tears ran down me cheeks, I did, but I could see she was upset, so I 'ad to tell the poor lass that yer cooks 'em whole!'

Dad and the young man shook with laughter. The story continued.

' "What?" says she. "Yon old granny told me 'ee 'ad to cut off the 'eads an' take out the innards, else 'eel be sick 'n' get the runs!" Well, I showed 'er that with no 'eads, tails or innards there weren't much left to eat, just a bit o' crispy skin. She says, "I'll never learn to cook! It's 'take the guts out o' this one, and leave the guts in another.'" "Yes," I tells 'er, "there's a lot more guts in a rabbit than there be in a sprat!" '

My father said he could just see it all, and he had a good laugh at the poor girl's expense. It was a good job, he said, that the young husband had such a gentle nature, as not many men would have been so forbearing.

Apart from wasting food she had wasted money, which was even worse.

'Come 'ome wi' me,' he said to Dad. 'It's only bread and cheese an' a bit o' pickle – she can't 'urt that!'

Dad agreed to go home with him for some supper, and they stopped outside the wagon which they had been given on their marriage. An identical one stood next to it. The young man said his wife's father had given it to them on the birth of their first child. Dad told us he could not help thinking about the struggle we always had to keep our heads above water. Just then, the wagon door opened and out squeezed an enormous woman. Dad said he could not stop staring at her. She was more than twice the size than when he had first seen her ten years earlier. Her beautiful features had disappeared into a mass of blubber, but her husband still looked at her as lovingly as the day they had wed. My father told my mother that they had it all, and two handsome sons.

'What more could a man want?' Dad asked.

'Perhaps a lovely daughter?' she suggested.

My father found it difficult to think of that lovely young woman as she had become in the ten years since he had seen her. She had looked like a glowing little flower back then. Mum made no comment, as she knew there were lots of reasons for getting fatter or thinner. Sure enough, Granny told my father that she had heard on the grapevine that the young bride had died at the age of just twenty-six. My mother and father went to the funeral. Someone said she had died of the dropsy. What a sad end for that lovely girl, who only had ten years or so with her husband. I can only imagine that they were very happy and eventful years.

Granny had the last word when travellers asked to pull in on her ground; Granfer never interfered. She rarely turned anyone away. Although we shared the same Romany background as the travellers, even in our eyes they were different. Their lives were very hard, as they were always being told to move on, often when they had only just set up camp.

The young woman who camped with us that year had a harrowing story to tell.

'The little ones were sobbin' with exhaustion, clingin' to me skirt. I was tryin' to breastfeed me baby, just a few weeks old, and they came an' told us to get on away, callin' us dirty Gyppoes, frightenin' the little ones even more.'

She caressed a small child as she spoke, and hitched up the baby on her hip.

'Me mother'd been bad fer weeks with the bronchitis. We managed to get a doctor who wouldn't take any money. 'E said me mother must go into the 'ospital where she would be warm 'n' cared fer, but Mam won't go. She thinks if she goes into 'ospital she's sure to die. We 'aven't got any money left.'

Grasping Granny's sleeve, she whispered, 'We ain't askin' fer money, but let us stay fer at least one night. They kicked our fire out an' the bit o' food we 'ad cookin' over it was trampled on by the police. We ain't 'ad nothin' to eat fer two days. I don't care fer meself,

135

but the chavvies are starvin'. Me 'usband went lookin' fer a bit o' grub an' 'e ain't back yet. 'Elp us, please.'

It would have taken a harder heart than Granny's to turn her down. But, Granny knew exactly what she was talking about. Just then her husband turned up, shocked to see his wife in such a state. He set to and built a couple of benders next to the wagon for his mother-in-law and the children. They had some of Granny's rabbit stew and then the children were washed. Still sobbing and clinging to each other, they lay down to sleep.

Their parents told Granny and Granfer what had been happening since they had married and had the children. They had been pushed from pillar to post, never knowing what the next day would bring. Jobs on the land were few and hard to find after the war. When they found work it was very poorly paid, and sometimes all they got was a few vegetables. The husband was living in fear because he had gone out early one morning once or twice and milked a cow so that his children would have at least some nourishment. He had been seen and chased by the farmer and his dogs, who had even let a shot off over his head.

'What else could I do?' he shrugged. 'I knowed I was doin' wrong, but me chavvies was starvin'.'

He looked half dead himself, and his poor little wife did not look much better. Granny let them stay, of course. There was no way she could let them leave in that state. She heard more of what they had suffered in the days that followed. We all sat around the camp fire listening to what sounded like a horror story. They had travelled the country, hoping and praying that they would be able to find somewhere where they would be allowed to stay. Even when his wife was in labour, they were told to move on. It was only after the intervention of a local doctor that his wife was able to deliver her child in peace. The very next day, however, they were made to leave.

Granny assured them that they could stay for a week or two, but even she could not help any more than this. She had been told by the local council that only a limited number of families could live on the land. We would all be in trouble if we allowed them to stay too long. Granny had had several battles with the council already, and she was not prepared to have any more.

'To 'ave a place where we could stay in peace is our dream,' said the wife. Granny soon put them straight, telling them about all the problems they had had with authority, that were ongoing.

'When I bought this ground, I didn't 'ave a penny left. We lived in a wagon an' a tent. When I tried t' make ower lives a bit better, we was told t' get off me own bit o' land. I thought we was safe 'ere, but they never left me alone. It took years afore I felt a little bit safe, but we still got t' be careful. I think Romanies like us will always be moved on by they who don't like nobuddy different. It's always been 'ard, but it's the life we chose, after all. The little ones depend on 'ee. 'Ee must do the best 'ee can fer 'em.'

The young husband's family did not want him to marry at all. They needed his help to support them all, but he was in love with a young Gypsy girl he had known since childhood. She and her widowed mother were really poor and lived in a tent and a home-made bender. With the help of the girl's mother, they got married. His family would have nothing to do with them, and constantly abused him for what he had done and accused him of betraying the family. Within a few weeks his wife was pregnant. They made another bender for themselves and one for the old lady. He had tried his best to find work, but they were close to starving and cold. They worked a few days at a time, picking beans, peas and potatoes, but they still had no decent shelter. Matters did not improve when a member of the family died and they witnessed 'the burning of the wagon'. How they must have felt seeing that wagon burn, when they had nowhere to live themselves! It sounds cruel and heartless but to Romany, that was the way it was.

The very next day their prayers were answered when one of their old uncles said they could have his old wagon, as he was going to live with his son who had married a *gadje* and lived on a smallholding in Wales. They jumped at the chance, and after a new coat of paint and a few repairs they had a nice little home. Now they thought everything would be all right. It was, for a few blissful days, but then it all started to go wrong. Everywhere they were stopped; they were abused and told to move on. If they went into a shop, they were eyed with suspicion. When the poor little wife gave birth, she managed with just the help of her mother, who was more scared than she was. The next day, they managed to get some help from the village midwife. She was a smiling, kindly woman who breezed into their lives only very briefly but who helped beyond measure.

'The baby's beautiful, love,' she said. 'What's she wrapped in?'

She unwrapped the baby from the husband's old shirt. Apart from a nappy, she was horrified to find that the baby had no clothes. She bathed the baby and handed her back to her mother.

'Right,' she said firmly, pointing a finger at the couple. 'On no account are you to move from here until I come back. I won't be long.'

She whisked out of the wagon and disappeared. Whether they stayed or not was out of their hands. They had already been given notice the evening before. But for once, things went their way. When the midwife returned she brought with her a pile of baby clothes, a basket of food and some milk. Overcome, they tried to tell her they had no money to pay her. She laughed.

'I'm not in the business of making money. A lot of mothers pass on their baby things to me so I can help someone who has nothing, or very little.'

She gently dressed the baby in the clothes, heated some milk for the new mum on the tiny stove and left the food, which included a whole roast chicken and would last for a few days. Then, with a kiss for the baby and a wave, she was gone, leaving them calling out their thanks. That was the only help they had, and thank God for that kind lass. Who knows what they would have done without her?

Since then, they had travelled the roads living in fear of what the next day would bring. When they finally packed up their wagon, Granny gave them a present of some food and milk for the children. They looked much better for their rest, and the little baby blossomed with all the attention she got from us children. They waved as the old horse plodded down the road. It was a sad sight to see them leave, and we watched until they disappeared around a bend in the road. Long after we still stood, wondering what was in store for them. It would not get any better for them, we all knew that, but at least they had a roof over their heads and hope in their hearts.

Granny knew what a hard fight they had on their hands, as she had endured more than most. Not many had Granny's strength of mind, or the ability to hold on when all seemed lost. We know with hindsight that things are still the same. Yes, you can buy your own land, but you cannot live on it as you like. 'Move on, move on!' You may well say, 'We're Romanies, it's our God-given right to travel if we wish, or stop if we wish.' But no, they say, 'You're tinkers, move on.'

Romany people, or *Roma*, have travelled the world for nine centuries, yet they are still treated badly, as if they have no right to live as they do. Romany people are not New Age travellers who adopt the life for their own reasons, perhaps seeing it as a romantic way of life or just wanting to opt out of the system. I expect they soon realise how hard it is to live life that way, with one set of problems being exchanged for another.

In the years before the Second World War there were some stopping places where Gypsies could rest for a while, usually during the winter. These were in the countryside on the outskirts of towns, but after the war, work in the hop fields dried up so many Gypsies were forced to settle. The trouble with this was that they still wanted to live the Romany way.

We were glad that Granny had the foresight to see what our lives would become if we kept travelling the roads, and bought her own land. At least we were able to get some education, and a certain amount of security from the knowledge that no one could move us on. Thank you, Granny and Granfer.

Love and War

In a corner of our big field was the air-raid shelter. This consisted of two old cars with the interiors gutted. In one was a mattress and bedding. Granny and Granfer slept in there if the siren went. The shelters were covered in hay, so as to look like a hay rick. I thought this was very clever, but I hated going in as it smelled damp and horrible.

The war almost seemed to pass our little haven right by. Of course, I knew there was a war on, but I had no idea what it actually was. All I knew was that I hated the approaching drone that meant planes would soon be flying overhead. If it was daytime, it would be the British on their way to Germany, and at night it would be the Germans flying towards Bristol or some other nearby town or city.

Often we would hear gunfire or loud bangs echoing in the distance, and my father would comment on how near or far away they might be. Hearing his voice, I was comforted and felt no fear. But I had a sense of foreboding when I heard the planes droning.

Sometimes the siren would go during the day, and whoever was at home would troop out to the shelter. We would huddle together until the all-clear sounded. My parents, however, would never go into the shelter, saying they preferred to take their chances in the open air. They never got out of their bed if the siren went at night, so soon after, I wouldn't either.

On one of the few occasions I did try to go to the shelter, I had been playing with some very heavy old curtain rings that my father had bought with some other junk. We had few toys, but these things were treasure to us. I had slid every one onto both arms from my shoulders to my wrists so they became bracelets. Suddenly the moan of the siren began. Startled, I tried to stand up, but overbalanced in my panic and from the weight of the curtain rings on my arms. I felt trapped. The rings weighted me to the ground, and I started screaming. With my noise, and that of the siren combined, my parents ran out. My mother saw me sitting in the dust, tear-stained and filthy, weighed down with the curtain rings. She could hardly pick me up, she was laughing so much. Sighing with relief, my father merely said, 'I thought the buggers had got you!' I never played with the curtain rings again. They probably made a good fire.

One day a man came to the school with lots of big square boxes. Inside were gas masks; black smelly rubber ones for the big children, and Donald Duck smelly ones for the smaller children. We were shown how to put them on and breathe in them, except I couldn't. I gasped and choked. All the other children seemed to be able to breathe in theirs, but I could not get the hang of it.

'Well then,' said the man who brought the gas masks, 'if there's a raid, you'll just have to die!'

Well, I thought to myself, I would rather die than put that filthy smelly thing on again. Anyway, by then the war was nearing its end and we hardly needed them. In any case, not one of us bothered to take them with us when we went to school or went out. To this day I hate the smell of rubber because of this.

We were very fortunate to live where we did, surrounded by wonderful countryside, rivers and streams, fields and lanes. It cost nothing, and we took it for granted most of the time, but we realised how much we appreciated it when we heard about the terrible things that were going on in the rest of the world. I was only aware of this when Mum took us to the pictures; a rare treat. We had settled down in our seats, absorbing the atmosphere in the cinema, our excitement highlighted by the music as the lights dimmed. We had enjoyed the first film, a comedy, when our attention was caught by some loud music. Suddenly a loud voice started shouting about the war. Images of burning houses flashed before us; people were running with terrified faces and smoke was everywhere. A small child lay bleeding in the gutter. It was this image that terrified me; it was too real. I had never seen anything like it in my short life. I thought that I would be burned, or left lying in the gutter. Mum had to take me home. She had thought it was a children's show, and that no news would be screened. I never forgot those scenes, and in years to come I was told that Hitler had killed many Gypsies. I felt I had had a very narrow escape.

My lovely Uncle Nelson was away fighting the war.
Once or twice when he was on leave he stayed a little
longer than he should have. Granny never minded.
When he was home, he would laugh and joke with her
and sing all the bawdy songs he had learned from his
soldier mates:

> She's me daughter, she's me daisy,
> She's cock-eyed and bloomin' lazy,
> She's got hairs upon her chest like any man;
> Ah! No matter where she goes
> Sure, everybody knows
> That she's Mick McGilligan's daughter Mary Anne.

'Oi! That's enough in front o' yer mother, m'lad!' she
scolded at some of the songs, but she secretly enjoyed
the fun.

The army sent the red caps one night to take him back
to the barracks. Their truck screeched up to the gate and
they quick-marched straight to Granny's hut.

'Right, where is he, then?'

Granny looked amazed.

'What? 'E went back days ago!'

'Are you sure about that, Mother?'

'I ain't yer mother! Yes, 'e's gone back.'

'He must've gone back barefoot, then,' observed the
sergeant. 'His boots are under that chair!'

Sure enough, Uncle Nelson had been caught red-
handed, or bare-footed. He came out from his hiding
place and gave himself up.

As we were already living in the country, there was no talk of evacuating us. Mum said that Gypsy families would never let their children go and live with strangers, even if strangers would have taken us in. I was very glad about that. We did have some evacuees at our little school, several boys and a few girls. The village children made their lives a misery at first. Bullying was rife among the boys. I felt quite sorry for them, but was also glad it was not me.

One girl was pale and thin-looking, and cried for her mother endlessly. Her eyes were constantly red-rimmed and her nose was always running. Sadly, no one wanted to know her. She looked clean enough, but her clothes smelled of cooking. I heard later that her clothes were hung behind the kitchen door where she was staying. Her mother came to our village for a while to make sure her little girl was all right, but she was shocked and upset to see the state her child was in. She wanted to take her home, but of course she was told not to, so she went home without her daughter, which made the child worse. My cousins and I tried to befriend her but no, while it was bad enough being an evacuee, in her opinion it was worse being a Gypsy. So we left her alone.

Some months later, a tall, sad-looking soldier came to collect her and we did not see her again, but we did hear from a teacher that her mother had been killed in an air raid. Poor little girl. I hoped that she would be happier at home, and at least she had her dad.

My mother thought it was a terrible thing to take

children as young as three from their families, and time has proved her right. We were relatively safe, not knowing what people in other parts of the country suffered. My own mother, whose sister Nancy lived in London, received a letter from Granny-in-Town informing her that Nancy had been killed in an air raid. We learned that she had gone out into the darkness to show off a dress she had made, to a friend who lived several streets away. Her friend's house had been bombed, and everyone in that street had been killed. Granny-in-Town had to go up to London, and identified her daughter by a small piece of the dress she had been wearing. Mum was broken-hearted at the news, and all she had of her much-loved sister was a silver brooch: a bar with the name 'Nancy' on it. I knew very little about my mother's sister Nancy. My mother rarely mentioned her, which did not mean that she was uncaring. She never dwelt on things she could not change, and with four small children to feed and clothe, she had plenty to keep her busy.

Mum grieved for her, but life still had to go on. I took the brooch one day, without asking, to pin my dress together as I had lost the button. I then lost it across the fields while picking blackberries. I was frightened to tell my mother as I knew she was still grieving, but I knew she would discover the loss eventually so I faced her with the awful truth.

'How would you feel if someone took something you valued and then lost it?' she demanded tearfully. I burst into tears of shame. Mum, who was rarely demonstrative, gave me a brief hug.

'Don't cry. It's gone now. You're more important than a brooch. I think some day someone will find it and think it's treasure trove!' she added.

The village where we went to school had some bomb damage, and sadly many lives were lost and homes were flattened. The only time the bombers came near us was when a plane was shot down in a nearby field. The crater it left was there for years, now grown over, and no one would ever guess at the young lives lost that night, or even give a thought for the mothers and fathers who grieved for their sons as the mothers and fathers in England grieved for theirs.

Our lives went on in the same old way they always had. By the time the war ended, I was seven years old. I went to a street party organised by our school and my Uncle Nelson came home for good. He had been badly wounded. Granny was horrified when she saw his scars. Hitler would not have stood a chance if she had had her way. Uncle Nelson was very quiet for a while, although as I was so young I did not notice the difference myself. He never once mentioned the war or his experiences. I can only think that the memories were so bad, he chose to forget. I think he would have preferred that the war had never happened.

Even his own children were unaware that his name was written on the Roll of Honour at the Memorial Hall in the village, until we had a family gathering there a while back and I showed them. They were both moved and amazed.

We children played often on the steps of the Memorial

Cross at the centre of our village, worn away by hundreds of childish feet. We felt no irreverence or disrespect, it was just somewhere for us to play. I like to think that the poor young men who died in the two terrible wars would have been glad to know how much we children enjoyed their memorial.

There was hardly any traffic back then. Cars were a great luxury, especially just after the war. Being in the scrap-metal business made it easier for Dad to acquire one at a good price and fix it up. He got an old Austin Ten, which he had to start with a starting handle. It was a sight to see on a frosty morning. He would wind the handle round and round as fast as he could and then stop, hoping to see if it would start. This would take quite a few turns, then suddenly the engine would burst into life and Dad would jump in quickly before the engine changed its mind and died.

It was a really old car when he got it. He had exchanged something else he had for it, and it drank up the petrol, so Dad only drove it at about ten miles an hour in the mistaken belief that this would save fuel. I thought it would have been quicker to walk than to have a lift with Dad. He was a very nervy driver, and would mutter about the other bad drivers all the way to school, or wherever he was going. The old Austin was so huge, my mother put the baby's pram in the back once and there was still plenty of room to sit down. There was a little roller blind on the back window, and little bud vases in which you could place a small spray of flowers. Dad only used the car about once a week to go to the pub or take us to school, but this was very rare.

On one occasion, he went out for a pint or two and left the car unlocked when he went into the pub. No one ever locked their cars in those days. He enjoyed his evening and then got into the car and drove home, singing to himself as he always did when he found himself alone. He pulled into the yard after two or three attempts, swearing profusely at the vehicle's inability to obey his instructions, such as 'Get into gear!' and 'Get on round there!'

Dad sat in the car for a minute or two while he recovered. Without warning, the back door clicked and swung open, and an extremely cultured voice spoke into Dad's ear.

'Thanks for the lift, old man, but try and mind your language next time!'

Swinging around in his seat, Dad was just in time to see a tramp vanishing out of the gate. Incensed, he jumped out of the car and followed him. He could just see him ahead in the moonlight.

'Next time yer wants a lift, just ask!' he shouted after the disappearing figure.

Dad laughed about it afterwards, though. He would have given the man a lift if he had asked. We think he must have climbed into the car to have a lift and fallen asleep while he was waiting.

There were many such homeless men in the late thirties and forties. Most of them were ex-servicemen who had lost everything and come home to nothing. Granny made most of them welcome, so I think they must have passed this knowledge on to their acquaint-ances, and this was the reason they felt they could make themselves at home.

In the very hot weather, the doors and windows of our wagon were left open. No one worried about strangers coming into the yard, as the dogs would have raised the alarm. It was a hot, sticky night and I could not sleep. I got out of my bed and made a little nest for myself in front of the open door. I lay for a while, breathing in the perfume of the night-scented stocks and watching the bright stars in the velvet sky. I must have dozed off because I awoke suddenly, my eyes still closed. I felt someone stroking my hair and lay still, thinking it was my mother, until a bad smell drifted past my nose. I knew instantly it was not my mother, and opened my eyes. Leaning over me was a tramp. I did not know if he was young or old as he had a massive beard and long, matted hair. More than that, he stank. I let out the loudest scream ever, so loud I woke the camp.

'What is it? What's the matter? Did somebody hurt you?'

I was not crying, but I was very frightened. Fear had gripped my vocal cords. When I could, I spoke in a small voice.

'I saw a tramp. He touched my hair and woke me up.'

Mum looked at my hair as though she could see where his hand had been.

'Why didn't the dogs bark?' she wondered. 'They wouldn't have let anyone in.'

I knew this to be true, and there was no sign of him now.

'You had a bad dream,' Mum sighed.

'No,' I said, 'I felt him touch my hair and I smelled him.'

Everyone went back to their beds. Dad went out and looked around for a bit, and then did the same.

The next morning, he went down the garden where there were some broken wires. It was a gap we children had made for a short cut. He came back holding a short stick on which he had impaled a filthy red hanky.

'What do 'ee make o' that, then?' he asked my mother.

She studied it for a minute.

'It's not anything I've ever seen before. It wasn't there last night when I fed the chickens. It looks like our Rosie didn't have a bad dream after all.'

'He did no harm,' said Dad, 'I'll mend the fence.'

No, he did me no harm, but I still remember the fright he gave me, and I dreamed of him for years. Even so, it was very strange that the dogs did not bark.

About this time, Granny got a lovely dog. He was part greyhound, and she called him Springer. She doted on him, and he in turn loved her and was her shadow, following her everywhere. He could perform all sorts of tricks. Granny would show him once, and Springer would perform.

One tramp came often. He was young and handsome, and we all wondered why he tramped the roads instead of staying home with his family. No one liked to ask, until one cold winter's day in 1947 Granny said he could stay in the wash house. There was an old armchair in there, and Granny said he could light the boiler to keep himself warm. He had a bit of supper and a cup of strong tea and then, poking the camp fire idly with a stick, he began to tell us his story.

'I had a wife and two children,' he began. 'I was away, fighting a war that nobody wanted.' He looked bitter.

'I was given a week's leave to spend at home with my family. I'd been waiting so long for that. So long . . .' He trailed off to take a sip of tea.

'When I got off the train, I saw a dreadful red glow in the sky. I could see by the moonlight that there was nothing left standing. The smell was terrible. I could hardly breathe. Suddenly, the siren sounded and I was pulled off the street and into a shelter. I thought to myself, hell must be like this. I could hear the noise of bombs dropping, screaming, shouting, clouds of dust . . . It was horrible.'

He shook his head, eyes closed, reliving the awful memories as we huddled together around the fire.

'It stopped as suddenly as it started. I started to walk towards my home but I could hardly recognise anything. An air-raid warden asked me where I was going and when I told him, he said, "Sorry, old man, the whole street was bombed a couple of days ago. There were no survivors."'

By now the tears were pouring down his cheeks. He sat up abruptly and wiped his face with the back of his hand.

'That's why I tramp the roads. I've nothing left. Nothing.'

Dad leaned forwards and touched his arm.

"'Ee's lost yer family. Would they want 'ee to give up? There's plenty to be done putting this country back on its feet. We 'ad a brother badly injured too. Me wife's sister died in the Blitz, but we 'ave to survive.'

He sat back and slapped his knee.

'If we give in, we're lettin' 'Itler win!'

We all went to bed that night feeling a little subdued. I glanced across to the wash house, watching the tramp slumped in the armchair, his face lit by the glow of the boiler.

In the morning he was gone, taking Granny's dog with him. She was angry, and said she wished she had not helped him now and had lost her dog because she had helped a stranger.

'Well, I don't s'pose the dog would've gone with 'im if 'e 'adn't wanted to,' said Dad.

We never saw the tramp again, or Granny's dog, but we heard tales of the clever dog who performed tricks for money outside pubs in the town, so perhaps we did help the tramp sort out his life. Granny missed her dog, and still looked for him years later even though she knew he must have died eventually. She even kept his bowl, in case he came back. Later on, Aunt Amy's youngest son Bobby got a dog who was almost Springer's twin. He was scarcely more than a pup, and Bobby decided to call him Springer, the same as Granny's dog. I expect he thought that the new Springer would somehow take the place of the first. But no, Granny never gave her affections that easily, and she never paid any attention to Springer number two. She saved any spare bones for him, but that was all. Springer number two was Bobby's dog. They went rabbiting together and spent long hours walking in the fields and lanes. When Bobby called, Springer came running. Bobby would open his arms and the dog would leap into them like a child returning home.

We saw many German and Italian prisoners of war, or POWs as they were called. The Germans mainly worked on the nearby farms. We weren't afraid of them, although I had the feeling we were meant to be, but I really preferred the handsome black-eyed Italians, as they were friendly to us children and sang and laughed while they worked. Granny shouted at one of them one day for stealing her daffodils. He looked very sad when she made him return them. I felt so sorry for him that I managed to sneak some to him later on. In return, he made me a pretty ring which I valued for years. To me, it was only a small thing to do for a man so many miles from home, who only wanted a little beauty in his life. I didn't consider him to be my enemy, and when they were finally sent home to their families, we missed them.

Rosina was one of my most favourite cousins. She was tall and slim with long, black wavy hair. In fact, Rosina decided a perm would make it even better. She could not afford to go to the hairdresser's, so she treated herself to a 'Pin-Up' home perm. She tried to read the instructions as best she could, and in spite of everyone begging her not to, she went ahead with her plan. The directions said, 'Leave the perm lotion on for five minutes.' Rosina thought that if five minutes was good, all night would be better.

She woke after a sleepless night and tried to remove the curlers. It was impossible. When, after several hands helping, she got them out, her hair was a broken, sticky mess. Rosina cried and cried. Finally, her sister had pity on her and took her to the hairdresser. A few hours later she came home smiling and sporting a very short cut, which suited her very well and she showed it off to everyone.

'You'd think that was what she wanted all along!' laughed my mother.

She was very young in her ways, although she was a few years older than me, and joined in any fun and mischief that was going. She made every occasion a success, and had an uncanny way of becoming the person she was talking to. She didn't seem to be able to stop herself. Often we would curl up with embarrassment.

There were always all sorts of interesting people visiting our yard, selling goods from suitcases. Many were from Europe or Asia. When they arrived, Rosina would rush out with a few shillings in her hand and start her bartering with, maybe, a turbaned Indian man. She would have the goods spread out all over the place in no time at all, and you could swear that she could speak his language. To his bemusement, she would jabber away, twisting scarves of different colours around her head and trying on every bangle.

'Pure silk, madam,' nodded the little man, who was by this time sweating freely.

'Get me my mother's wedding ring!' Rosina cried. 'I'll test it!'

She had heard that if you can pull a scarf through a wedding ring, it proves that the fabric is pure silk. Rosina was eager to test the theory out. By now she was trying on a pink satin blouse over an old jumper, resulting in a huge tear under the arm. By the time someone had brought out the wedding ring, she had been distracted by a brightly coloured ring the pedlar had in his suitcase. She forced it on to the smallest finger she had and then realised she couldn't get it off. (She wore it for weeks after, her finger getting greener and greener until the ring finally broke and she was free of it.) She paid for nothing, saying the ring was broken, as indeed it was, weeks later. Chattering away at this poor Indian pedlar in what she believed was his language, she strolled off in the silk scarves. Granny tried to placate him as he stumbled out of the gate and away on his bike. He must have been a glutton for punishment, as he returned many more times only to have Rosina repeat the same performance. My father did try to stop her, but gave up in the end, saying, 'The man must know our Rosina by now.'

She behaved in a similar fashion towards the French onion seller. He too arrived on a bike, his beret perched on the side of his head. He was tanned, with a small moustache and all his strings of onions hung from the handlebars. Rosina soon divested him of the strings of onions and the beret, and was at once transformed into a female French onion seller. She went to all her aunts and cousins, selling them the onions and collecting the money for the Frenchman. It was hilarious watching her performance. She wiggled her hips, snapped her fingers and blew kisses to all and sundry. The onion seller returned many times, as he was quite taken with her, but Rosina was as innocent as a child and only had one true love.

Lots of Germans stayed on after the war, and Rosina fell in love with one of the farm workers. His name was unpronounceable to any of us, so all who knew him called him 'Bob the German'. Rosina had a great love for all that was foreign and mysterious. To her, a young man who spoke to her in a different accent, after being brought up in a small community in Somerset, was the epitome of exotic. When Granny and Granfer noticed her strange behaviour, they soon deduced that Rosina was in love. When they discovered who she was in love with, there was much to argue about.

"E ain't yer own kind!' growled Granny to a scowling Rosina.

"E be a *gadje*!' Granfer choked.

He was also short, pale and skinny with a Hitler moustache. My mother could not believe that beautiful, dark-eyed Rosina could fall in love with what my father called 'a weasel of a man'!

Rosina would not be moved. She was in love with Bob the German, and she told me so.

'He winked at me, Rosie!' she exclaimed excitedly one day. 'An' I winked back!'

So that was it. Granny tried hard to put every obstacle in her way. Bob was told never to set foot on Granny's land, so Rosina sneaked off at every opportunity to meet him elsewhere. She went for long walks in the countryside and into town to the pictures. She was about sixteen at this time, still very young, and I was a very young nine-year-old confidante to her. It was I who she drew aside one spring day into the secretive cover of the old wash house.

'Rosie! Come yer a minute. I got something real important to tell 'ee!'

She glanced around furtively. I sensed something unusual in the way her eyes flashed with a mixture of fear and excitement.

'Promise me! Promise me 'ee won't tell *anybody* what I'm tellin' 'ee now!'

'Tell what?' I shrugged. I had no idea of the import of what came next.

'Swear! Say, "God's honour!"' she commanded.

'God's honour.'

She took a deep breath and gripped my shoulders.

'I'm runnin' away, Rosie! I'm going to London with my Bob and we're gettin' married! But don't 'ee tell a soul! 'Ee won't now, will 'ee?'

Her eyes frantically seached mine for confirmation.

'No, 'course I won't.'

She relaxed her grip and whisked away into her wagon. By the time I went to bed I had completely forgotten what she had said.

I was awoken the next morning by a lot of raised voices mixed with hushed ones. She was gone, and everyone was looking for her except me. I just kept quiet as they searched all day for her. Finally their concerned faces forced me to say something, and I casually remarked to my mother that she had gone to London to get married. All hell broke loose. I was in big trouble. I should have been frightened, I think, but as a young child I was not overly worried about what Rosina had done, being totally oblivious to the possible consequences. Having led such a sheltered life, how could I? I was only sad because Rosina was leaving. My mother broke the sorry news to my aunt and uncle, and I was frogmarched before them to explain every detail of what I had been told. I was asked the same question over and over again.

'Why didn't you tell us, if you knew?'

I could only reply that I had promised not to. Well, it was too late by then. Rosina was married, had her family and eventually moved to Germany.

Working to Live

My father and his brothers were general dealers, and they bought scrap metal from whoever wanted to sell. It was hard and dirty work with very poor rewards, but it was an honest living. The scrap was kept in one large heap in the centre of the field to the left of the gate, between and behind Aunt Betsy's place and my Aunt Brit and Uncle Tom's place.

They bought and sold old cars, carts, ancient tractors and farm implements that had long since been useful; in fact, anything you could think of. Cars were few and far between at that time, and you never saw a washing machine or fridge among the twisted, rusting metal. They spent hours saving everything that could be saved, reusing anything that could be reused, getting tired and filthy in the process. Nothing was ever wasted. On Fridays, the scrap would be slung onto the back of the old lorry and taken to the big scrap yard.

I used to watch in fascination as Dad collected all the tiny bits of scrap lead in a special pot, and heated it over the fire until it melted. When it had cooled and set hard, he would turn it out like a jelly. It would weigh several pounds and would sell for a good price, as did copper and brass. When Dad bought an old bus for scrap, we children had the time of our lives. It was towed into the yard to its final resting place. Upstairs and downstairs, we were princes and princesses; we played houses and made pretend kitchens for many happy hours. The day we saw Dad and my uncles breaking up our lovely bus, we knew it had to be, and straight away we centred our attention on an American jeep. Then we were in the army looking out for the enemy. We had so much fun in those old cars, playing for hours on end with seldom a falling-out.

One day, they brought some big boxes home stuffed with army and air force uniforms. We all dressed up in these, hats, jackets and everything. We must have looked a sight, but we thought we looked like film stars. We played with these for weeks, and were the envy of the children at school. Other items in the boxes included small periscopes. What fun we had seeing the world from a different angle.

Another time, they brought home lorryloads of boxes, possibly for ammunition as they were double thickness and packed with an oily substance which looked like wax, and which we used as moulding dough. The boxes were held together by hundreds of brass screws. This was the real treasure. A huge bonfire was made, and the wonderful boxes burned! The fire burned all day and all night, but after it had died and the ashes were cold, Dad and my uncles patiently sieved the ash to collect every single brass screw. When they had finished, they had a substantial weight in scrap brass worth a few hundred pounds. That was a great day for us all, and the money lasted several months.

All money earned was split three ways. Working life was very hard and I cannot imagine that they made much money, but we survived. Mum did her bit for their business by filling in their insurance forms and dealing with the tax for their lorries. She read all the letters that came to Granny or anyone else in the camp that needed help. Mum was clever, and her advice was often sought by my cousins and aunts in that way.

Dad's was very dirty, oily work, and Mum had her own cut out to keep up with all the washing, especially as at that time all the water had to be fetched from the river bucketful by bucketful. Mum would rub a little lard into her hands after doing the washing to relieve the soreness but they never really healed, so when Dad brought home The Washing Machine she was overjoyed. It was a strange-looking object, with a sort of paddle that had to be pulled back and forth. It was not electric, so the water it used had to be heated in the old boiler as before, making it just as much hard work. Mum faithfully used it several times before an audience of aunts and cousins, but it took twice as long.

'That's it!' she announced, hands on hips. 'I won't be using *that* again!'

'You must be using it wrong. I'll show 'ee 'ow it's done,' said Dad.

'Well, if it gets the washing looking clean and bright as before, like the old boiler, I'll use it,' Mum agreed, confidently holding up her grey whites. Dad showed her how the very next morning, manfully paddling away, but everyone could see that the washing was dirtier than ever. No, she would never use it again. Everyone had a go, and agreed that it was worse than useless.

'Sell it for scrap,' Mum suggested, as Dad scratched his head. So Dad put it up on the old lorry and sold it for scrap. Mum went back to her old way of washing by hand and was happier for it.

The men worked hard at everything they did, with no machines to help them break up the scrap metal. Everything had to be done by hand. We could hear them banging and hammering away until late at night. The next day it would all be piled on the old lorry and sold for whatever price they could get. I can still see them sitting around the camp fire, Dad with his trilby pushed to the back of his head with a mug of thick dark tea in his hand. Sometimes they earned good money, other times not so good, but Dad was always in charge of sharing it around. They each got an equal amount in notes, but if there was any 'silver' left over, he would say, 'That's mine. I got chillun to look after.' This was completely acceptable to the others. If Dad had a good week, he would give my mother several pounds more than usual. He knew that she would put some away for the times when he did not earn so much. She was a good manager, but often bad week followed bad week, and then there would be no more left in the pot. It was during those times that we would be more than glad of a dish of Granny's stew or a broth with a thick hunk of bread.

My family never claimed any benefits from the government. Some said we never paid taxes as we should, but then we had none of the services that house dwellers were used to. We had no waste collections, so we burned what could be burned; anything else was composted or fed to the chickens, and any tins went into the scrap pile. Larger items were taken to the town dump on the lorry. We had no gas or electricity. For many years we had no running water, so every drop we used was carried from the river. We had to cross two fields to reach it, and traverse the riverbank which was very steep – and often muddy – in order to fill a bucket. It was no fun trudging through muddy fields with water slopping in your wellies. Many times we returned soaked and freezing, and to make matters worse, there would only be a few inches of water left in the bucket. Summers were better, though; we loved being sent to get the water as we would take the dogs and let them have a swim further down the river. By the time we got home, hours had passed and Mum was still waiting for her water.

It was a red-letter day, then, when the powers that be decided we could have running water. This arrived in the form of one single standpipe to be shared among all the families. This was housed in a little three-sided wooden shelter. You wouldn't have thought this a luxury, but it was to us! Fresh water on tap! Well, we could now have a cold drink without having to boil it and wait for it to cool first. Believe me, water from an outside tap tastes far better than boiled. All of us children wasted a lot of this precious commodity in the next few days, revelling in the novelty. We let it run away and squirted each other until Granny put a stop to it. The trouble was, every winter it would freeze solid. My Uncle Alfie would pack old newspapers around the pipe and set fire to it to try and defrost it. Sometimes it worked. Other times the pipe burst, so all in all it was a mixed blessing.

Once, I truly did believe I had found treasure. I was trying to catch tiddlers in the ditch that ran between our wagon and the wheat field behind. It had been raining on and off for weeks, and the water in the ditch looked quite clean for once. Lying on my belly, I gazed into the water. Suddenly, the sun came out from behind the clouds and I saw something glinting in the shallows below me. I picked up a twig and started poking about in the water, and quickly hooked out what looked like a necklace. It was made of rows of tiny little beads that appeared to be brass metal joined together with tiny chains. I hooked up three or four of what I thought were necklaces made of brass. They did not appeal to me, and no one I knew would ever wear brass, so I threw them back in the muddied water. Some years later, I mentioned it to my father. To my surprise, his jaw dropped and he gazed at me in horror.

'Why didn't you tell me at the time?'

'Why?' I shrugged. 'It was just rubbish.'

'I don't think so. I reckon those beads were gold! If they'd been brass, they would've turned black. Were the ones you found black?'

'No, Dad. They were bright 'n' shiny – just a bit broken.'

Dad closed his eyes and looked as though he would burst into tears.

Me aged two on the wagon steps.

My dear mother, aged twenty-eight.

My father, smiling as usual.

Mary Ann, my wonderful granny.

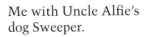
Me with Uncle Alfie's
dog Sweeper.

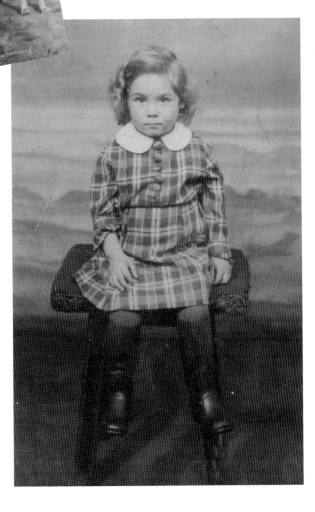

e having won
e wellingtons
ır.

My cousins.

My first school photo, age four and a half.

My last school photo, age fourteen.

Edwin my dear granfer with some of his children and grandchildren

'Rosie,' he said slowly, 'I'm pretty sure that the beads you found must've bin gold.'

I cannot say that I felt very bothered by this supposition. I knew gold was valuable, but so were brass and copper. Dad and my uncles often spoke about the cost of those commodities as our living depended upon it, but I had only ever seen it in its scrap form, twisted and broken. Dad went out immediately and searched, digging deep in the ditch, but found nothing but mud and weeds. Looking back now, the more I think about it, the more sure I am that they were gold. I can still see them hanging on the end of my stick, glinting in the sun. Well, it was too bad. We never had any money, and maybe we could have been rich but what you never had you never miss. I expect the necklaces are still there now, buried deep in the mud, hidden and secret.

My father and uncles travelled miles to fetch a few bits of metal or an old scrap car, coming home not to a bathroom with hot and cold running water but to a big black kettle boiled on the camp fire. They did their best to keep clean, but it was not easy. I can still see Uncle Alfie sitting down by the fire in his oily clothes, enjoying a mug of tea before having a wash, his bright blue eyes and his white teeth gleaming in his oily face. I loved to read the poem on the side of his mug, which read:

> Let the wealthy and great
> Roll in splendour and state

I envy them not, I declare it,
I eat my own lamb, chicken and ham,
I shear my own sheep and I wear it.
I have fields, I have flowers,
I have trees, I have bowers,
The lark is my morning alarmer,
So jolly boys now, God speed the plough,
Long life and good health to the farmer.

When the crops had to be planted or harvested, the men had to help with this before and after a hard day's work. Their arms were strong and muscular because of this, but they accepted their lot without complaint and we kept our heads above water.

Granfer brought many strange things back from the markets. Sometimes he bought items of furniture which Granny took a fancy to and kept for herself. The rest Granfer sold, or, if it was too battered or worn, he would use it for firewood. Granny acquired several wooden armchairs this way, which were extremely comfy. When Granny first had them, they most likely would have had a glossy coat of varnish or polish, but after Granny had had a few goes at them with her trusty scrubbing brush, they would be as white as the top of her kitchen table. Granny would be well pleased, because to her they were clean, and that was more important to her than the way they looked.

Cleanliness was all that Granny required to make her happy. She wasted many hours in the pursuit of cleanliness. With the many menfolk in and out of her hut in their dirty work clothes and the scarcity of water, it was hard to achieve, but she never stopped trying. It was the same with the rugs that Granfer bought for just a few shillings. These rugs were brightly coloured and patterned, with long fringed edges. Early in the morning, Granny would get my father to fill the boiler with water and get the fire going beneath to heat it up. Meanwhile, she would collect every rug she could carry and spread them flat on the wash-house floor and then throw buckets of hot soapy water over them. Then, taking hold of a hard broom, she would scrub each one to within an inch of its life.

When she felt they were clean enough, she would dip a small bowl into the buckets of fresh water that had been collected for her and rinse each rug clean of dirty, soapy water, and then spread them over the hedges that surrounded her land to dry in the sun. In the summer this did not take too long, but in the winter it could take weeks. Sadly, when they were dry, they would have lost any vestige of their former colours, and each would have become a dull shade of beige or brown. This did not bother Granny. The fact that they were clean and fresh was all that mattered to her; besides, Granfer could always get more, as they cost very little at the market. Granny always felt better after a morning's scrubbing. Yes, she always scrubbing something, was Granny.

The best thing that Granfer ever brought home was a throne. Well, it was not a real throne, but we thought it was. It had a tall back with lots of carving, and the seat and back were upholstered with red velvet. Prissy and Rosina often fought over who would sit on this chair, and would dress up in old net curtains, home-made crowns and bunches of paper flowers and parade around like royalty.

'I be the Queen, I'm the tallest. You be the King, you looks more manly, like.'

'No, I don't! I don't look manly! Don't say I do!'

'Well, I've got long curly 'air, like that there queen 'ad in that book we 'ad read to us by the teacher.'

So it would go on. When Granfer announced that he was going to sell the chair and that we could not play with it any more, we argued and pleaded, but for once he would not be moved.

'No. I got a feller comin' to fetch it, an' 'e's already paid me fer it.'

Our disappointment was tempered by the fact that we realised we could have one last game with it. Surely one more game would not hurt. We waited until Granfer had gone out with the horse and cart and we pulled it out of the corner of the wash house, where Granfer had hidden it. We pulled the covers off, and there was the beautiful chair in all its throne-like glory. Who could resist? We had played with it many times before, and no harm had come to us. Someone commented on the little piles of sawdust underneath the chair, but we took no notice as none of us knew what it meant. We played kings and queens and ladies-in-waiting for an hour or more before returning it to where it had been and covering it up carefully. A week later it was collected by its new owner.

'Don't bother uncovering it. I've seen that it's all right. In any case, I'm putting it into storage for a twelvemonth,' he explained as he and Granfer loaded it onto the back of a cart. We watched it go, thinking how much we would miss our throne, and the many games we could have played on it. We soon forgot it, though, and went on to play with something else.

Many months later, when we had all forgotten about the lovely chair and Granfer had spent the money, the man and his sons came back. Granfer raised his hat to him.

'Good mornin'.'

'I'll give you "Good morning!" ' he growled. 'Give me back my money! If I'd wanted firewood, I'd have bought it for pence, not pound notes!'

Granfer was truly mystified, as were the rest of us.

'Don't 'ee talk t' me like that!' said Granfer. 'I ain't sold 'ee any firewood!'

The man was fairly foaming at the mouth, and he lurched forward to grab Granfer but Granfer was too quick and stepped back, causing the man to fall to his knees in the dust. Granfer, being the gentleman he was, bent down and offered his hand to help him up.

'Don't make out that you don't know what I'm talking about!' the man shouted at Granfer.

'But I don't!' replied Granfer, looking perplexed. 'Why don't 'ee tell me, then I can answer 'ee!'

By now, everyone who was at home was gathered around, wondering what all the fuss was about.

'Don't all of you look surprised?' the man yelled. 'All of you are in on it!'

In on what? we all wondered. He turned on his son.

'Bob! Get that sack bag!' he demanded. Bob fetched the bag and his father opened it and emptied the contents in the dust before Granfer. We all stared at what looked like a lot of firewood, but then I recognised the pieces of red velvet. What was that doing in this pile of old wood? We were all totally bemused. Granfer bent down and poked at the wood, and it crumbled and dry sawdust flew into the air.

'That,' said the man, arms akimbo, 'is the valuable chair that I paid you sixty pounds for back last year.'

The look of shock and incredulity on all our faces got through to the man at last. He must have known that we had no idea the chair was full of woodworm when Granfer sold it. He had not taken the trouble to unwrap it when he got home, and had put it in storage with his other stuff that he hoped to sell for a profit. Meanwhile, the woodworm had had a party. The wonderful chair that had given us so many hours of fun was now fit for the fire. Not only that, but he said the other pieces of furniture had been ruined as well. And he would have to spend pounds treating it, and may not be able to sell it with worm holes in it. We were all shocked and sorry that our throne had ended up in splinters. Granfer tried to apologise, to no avail.

'I don't want "sorry", I want to know what you are going to do about it!'

'What dost 'ee mean? I can't make 'ee another chair. 'Ee bought it in good faith, an' I sold it to 'ee in good faith. I asked 'ee if 'ee wanted to look at it again, an' 'ee said "No". If 'ee 'ad o' looked, 'ee might o' seen the worms then. I seen no sign.'

The man flew at Granfer in a towering rage. He could

not speak for temper. His sons grabbed his arms and held him back.

'It's no good, Dad,' said Bob. 'Best get home and clear out the shed.'

'I'll have the law on you!' said the man. 'You wait and see!'

'I'm sorry,' said Granfer, 'everybody 'ere is sorry, but I can't give 'ee thy money back. It's long gone. And why should I? Thee's the expert. 'Ee should've 'ad a look when I told 'ee to.'

Well, it was left like that for the time being. The man and his sons drove off in a temper. Granfer scratched his head and turned to us little ones.

'Did 'ee see any sign o' worms in that there chair?'

We shook our heads. We did not know what he meant, and I was imagining the worms that we dug up in the garden.

'We did see some little piles of sawdust but nothing else,' I suggested, innocently.

'Where were these little piles of sawdust?' Dad asked carefully.

We all ran to the wash house, to where the little piles of dust remained undisturbed. We stood around in silent anticipation. Suddenly, Dad let out a bellow of laughter, and Granfer followed suit. Pretty soon we were all in fits, but only Dad and Granfer knew what we were laughing at. Dad kept on gasping and slapping his knee, repeating, 'Little piles of sawdust! Little piles of sawdust!'

Of course, the woodworm must always have been in the chair, maybe hidden by the velvet upholstery. It was a good job we had not mentioned the sawdust piles earlier, or Granfer would have been in trouble for selling faulty goods. Instead, he was completely innocent, and we never saw the man again.

It seemed as though the wonderful chair was only meant for us to enjoy. The fairy-tale stories that we had performed had disintegrated into dust when it was taken away from children who had no other playthings, but who still managed to squeeze every bit of fun out of ordinary, or, in the case of our chair, extraordinary things.

Our possessions were few, but we looked after what we had. My dad owned two shirts, one shabby suit, one pair of 'decent' shoes and one pair of old boots for working in. He always wore a tie for 'best', of which he had one. But rain or shine, he always wore a trilby hat, and of these he had two; an old one for everyday and again, a new one for best – weddings and funerals.

He looked so good in a trilby that the owner of the shop where he bought them gave him two hats one day, because he said Dad was a wonderful advertisement for him. So Dad chose a brown one for winter and a grey one for summer. He did look good in them!

Mum had strung a washing line up just outside the caravan door to hang our socks out to dry for school. Dad came home that evening after having his usual pint at the pub. On entering the doorway, he handed Mum two little socks and a hanky. He fell into fits of laughter as he told us he rode the bus into town with people looking at him and smiling all the way to the pub. He hadn't minded, as he thought everyone was admiring his lovely new hat. It was only when he got to the pub and someone asked him what he had on his hat that he realised he had been on the bus and walked all through town with the socks and hanky draped over his smart new hat!

My father kept ferrets. They were beautiful creatures, with creamy-coloured fur. Rosina hated and feared them, and they were the nemesis of her nightmares. They were very tame, though, and Dad kept titbits from his meal for them. They always seemed to know when he was near, even when he had just got off the bus, which stopped some yards down the road. They set up such a noise, calling and squealing, until Dad gave them their treat. They certainly smelled bad, even though they were kept very clean.

Dad, Granfer and one or two of the younger boys would go poaching. Even though people were hungry for meat this was a crime, punishable by a heavy fine. Dad and Granfer thought it was worth the risk to feed our large extended family. They used the ferrets and nets to catch the rabbits, and there were so many of them that Dad never came home empty-handed. Many a good meal was eaten and enjoyed courtesy of the farmer.

My father often told the story of how, on one of those nights, he stood up to his waist in water in a ditch, hiding from him. It was a moonlit night, but a bramble bush hid him from the farmer's sight. Dad said he was only a few inches away from this farmer, who kept his gun cocked while he shouted threats into the air.

'I can see thee!' he bellowed. 'Dirty thief! I'll see thee in jail! Get off my land!'

A twig cracked and he swung around violently, stumbled backwards and let off a shot which whistled just past Dad's ear, knocking his trilby off in its flight. Dad said, how he did not shout out, he would never know. The farmer must have thought he had killed someone as he stumbled away, still uttering threats in a very shaky voice. Dad stood in the cold water a little while longer until all was quiet. Slinging the rabbit around his neck, he started to look for his hat, but he could not find it in the darkness and sorrowfully decided it had sunk.

When he arrived home, Mum realised that if Dad's hat was found he would be caught, as no one locally wore a trilby like his. Most men wore caps, even the farmers. Dad quickly reassured Mum.

'Don't worry. It'll be hidden by the brambles, or sunk. Anyway, I knows what to say if the coppers come.'

It had to be left at that. Dad seemed completely unperturbed. Later on that day, the farmer came for Dad and the village policeman was with him. The constable looked a little embarrassed, clearing his throat and running his fingers around his collar. It was not surprising to Dad, as many a free rabbit the policeman and his family had enjoyed, no questions asked.

'Hello!' smiled Dad, as they entered our yard.

'Don't you "hello" me!' choked the farmer. 'You wuz on my land last night, poachin' my rabbits!'

Dad looked the picture of innocence.

'Not me,' he said. 'I wuz abed. I 'eard a shot, though.'

'Yes, you 'eard a shot all right, cuz you wuz there!'

Like a conjuror at a children's party, he produced Dad's old trilby hat with a piece missing from the brim. He swung it to and fro before Dad's face.

'Don't say this ain't yourn! I sin yer wearin' it enough!'

Dad stared at the farmer in mock pity, and pointed to his head.

'Don't be daft, man,' he laughed. 'I'm wearing me old brown trilby!'

The farmer nearly choked with rage.

'I don't care! No, I don't care! This hat's yourn and you know it!'

'Prove it,' said Dad, 'and I'll still say it ain't mine! I've got two hats – one grey and one brown. You can tell this hat's old. I've never had three.'

At this point, the constable touched the farmer on the arm.

'Come along, you'll never be able to prove it.'

At that moment, Dad said he believed that the farmer would have given all he possessed to prove Dad a thief. With the policeman holding his arm, he stumbled away, looking back and shaking his head in disbelief. Dad watched him go.

'How on earth did you do that?' Mum asked, incredulously. Tapping his nose, Dad took her to the old shed where he kept all his useful odds and ends. Pulling out an old sack, he tipped out several old and battered trilby hats. Mum gasped and put her hand to her mouth. She thought he had thrown all his old hats away, but she was glad that he had not. They had certainly got him out of a lot of trouble, at least for now.

Dad, however, thought he had lost his ferrets as he had left them behind in his flight. He was saddened because they were his friends, but sneaking back later on, he called them softly. To his astonishment, a few minutes later, they stuck their heads out of a burrow. Dad quickly popped them in his pocket and went home happy.

As a child, I could never understand why farmers were not willing for anyone, especially 'Gyppoes', to snare rabbits on their land. No harm was ever done to the land; indeed, years later, picking blackberries on a warm September day, I counted eight or nine rabbits, some dead, others dying with the horrible man-inflicted myxomatosis. Many people back then would have willingly given sixpence for a rabbit to feed their children, but the powers that be preferred to give them that terrible disease to control their numbers. I hope I never have to see that again. Although I enjoyed many a plate of rabbit stew, I knew I could not eat it any more. Thank heaven someone came to their senses and stopped that dreadful practice.

Dad saw the farmer in the pub some weeks later. He glared at my father bitterly.

'I've sin yer, acting the nob with yer posh 'ats! I know 'twas you a-poachin' my rabbits,' he muttered into his cider. 'Yes, I know for certain 'twas you, acting the gentry in yer fancy 'ats. I'll be lookin' out for you!'

Dad only laughed.

'You go 'ome, old chap, and eat till you bust. Don't

you worry if other folk starves, so long as you're all right!'

Dad was right about the farmer. He was the personification of the typical jolly farmer, except he was not in the least bit jolly.

A few weeks later, Dad was walking home from the pub early one evening. He told us he was tired after working hard all day on one of the local farms. As he passed a field, he happened to glance across and saw the same farmer apparently asleep in a haystack. Dad passed on by, but then started to worry and wondered whether or not he might be asleep or drunk. He knew the farmer was fond of his cider, and maybe a bit too much. It started to rain, so Dad thought he would just check to see if the old chap was all right. He shook him and called his name, but whatever he did, he could not wake him. Dad realised that he was very drunk. Looking around, he spotted an old wooden barrow. With a struggle, Dad got him in and started for home. It was not easy as he was getting even more tired, and several times he tipped the old chap out into the lane.

Eventually he got him home and knocked loudly on the door. It was opened by a child.

'Here's yer dad. Best get yer mother,' he said, pointing to the laden barrow. He looked over his shoulder as he walked through the gate and, watching him in amazement, saw a crowd of women and farm hands with several giggling children. He laughed to himself all the way home.

'You should've left the old misery there!' my mother said drily. 'If that'd been you drunk in the haystack, he would likely have put a bullet through you and said you'd been poaching!'

A few days later, however, we found a brace of rabbits and a brace of pheasants on the caravan steps. We knew who had left them there, but he would never have admitted it.

Bringing the Harvest Home

*I*n the spring we spent all day outside. There was always lots to do. My father planted his potatoes around Easter, as he said that was the best time. Peas and runner beans were planted a little later. Both he and my uncles knew all about leaving the land fallow, but they did not have enough land to spare a whole field, so they just left a wide strip in a different part of the field each year. This seemed to work very well, as the crops always gave a good yield. I remember my father using a horse-drawn plough. He was very good at it, and I loved to see the rich brown furrows peeling away from the plough.

'Every one as straight as a die!' as Dad would say. When he was finished, he would wipe his forehead on his shirtsleeve and gaze with pride on his achievement.

'Not everybody can do that, Rosie,' he would say. 'If 'ee can't do it, don't try and learn it!'

In later years, when the horses were gone, they would ask one of the farmers to plough the field for them. No money changed hands, as Dad or one of his brothers would work a day or so in exchange to pay for it. This suited everyone and continued for many years, the land feeding us and bringing in a little money.

Granny and Granfer sold the produce from door to door, and many people stopped and bought at the gate. They usually came back for more as the vegetables were as fresh as a daisy, having only just been picked. If Granfer weighed them up, he was very generous with his measures, especially if he had just had a tot of whisky. Sometimes he would not bother to weigh their veg, but throw a large handful into their bags.

'Just give me thruppence, my maid,' he would say to whichever young woman he was serving. If he was feeling really happy, he would give them a bunch of sweet peas as well. No wonder his sons all said that everything went whenever Granfer sold the vegetables, but there was never any money in the cash box!

One vegetable Granfer had plenty of was marrows. I used to wonder why he grew them because every one of us hated them. When they were cooked it was like eating nothing, and they disintegrated into a horrible mush that even the dogs just sniffed at and walked away from.

One day, Mum gave us something very nice for our supper. We asked what it was, but she would not tell us until we had cleared our plates.

'It's only marrow,' she said.

We did not believe her. It was much too nice to be marrow. How did she make a horrible mushy vegetable taste so good? She explained.

'First, you have to peel the marrow and remove all the

seeds, then you mince up what was left from the meat we had for Sunday dinner' (I expect it was rabbit), 'and then you mix it all up with breadcrumbs, chopped onion, sage and thyme from the garden, and you season it with salt and pepper and a little chopped wild garlic. Then fill up the space where the seeds were removed, put the other half of the marrow back on and cover it with the paper wrappers kept from the butter and just cook it in a hot oven until it's ready.'

Mum only had the small range to cook on and no thermostat to regulate the heat but the result was delicious. I well remember this recipe and have tried it myself many times, but my efforts never tasted like my mother's.

Autumn is my favourite time of year. The weather is often warm and sunny. Those were the days when we picked pounds of blackberries. Most were sold to the blackberry man, and some of the best we gave to Mum for jam, which we all loved. Like many women during the war, Mum made some strange concoctions to make food go further. Most turned out fine, and we ate and enjoyed them immensely. Someone gave her a recipe for marrow, carrot and ginger jam. We all thought it would taste horrible but we had very few sweet things, and Mum said she could add some saccharin to make the sugar go further. We did protest at this, as we all hated the taste of saccharin. However, Mum stuck to her guns and, collecting a marrow, carrots and a small bit of ginger, made her jam. It boiled away for ages and smelled lovely. We all lined up for a taste as soon as it was cool. I can honestly say I have never tasted anything so revolting in my life. Mum was so disappointed.

'What does yours taste like?' I asked her. She had another taste and replied solemnly, 'Like nothing on earth!' We laughed until our sides ached, but then Mum's face straightened again.

'Well, I can't waste good food, it will have to be eaten up.'

We could not believe our ears. Surely she did not mean it. She must be joking. But no, she meant every word. Over the course of about a year, the jam was eaten. Mum tried to disguise it in many ways, but it still tasted vile. My father dropped a jar once, 'By accident,' he said. Judging by the massive wink he gave us, however, I doubted it. After that, she made jam with the usual fruit and this was always delicious, but we never forgot the marrow jam.

She did try another recipe with cubed marrow, cooked for about a minute in lemon juice and a bit of sugar, allowed to cool overnight and then dished up for our supper with a bit of evaporated milk. This was supposed to taste like melon. I can only say that whatever else it tasted like, it was definitely not melon. None of us could eat it. It was utterly disgusting. Mum, bemoaning the fact that she had wasted sugar and evaporated milk, threw it to the chickens, who would not eat it either. So it lay in the dust of the chicken run, reproaching Mum for days until it finally rotted away. If ever she suggested that she was going to try out a recipe someone had told her was delicious, we all yelled at once, 'No! Remember the "melon!" ' Little Christopher would join in, 'No! No memon!' which made us laugh.

Everything my mother cooked we ate and enjoyed, probably because we knew how much effort had gone into every dish. The little stove was the bane of her life, and the only thing we could be sure of was toast, so Mum was always glad when the salad vegetables were in season.

We loved Mum's roast potatoes, which she cooked around whatever meat she had. The taste and wonderful flavour of those richly coloured roast potatoes linger in my memory. We did not have fancy food, but I know my mother was a wonderful cook, and she did wonders with what she had. Most of all we loved her rabbit stews, which were a weekly event without fail. We would come home from school, and on entering the yard we would recognise the wonderful smell. Talk about 'the Bisto kids' – they had nothing on us!

Mum would soak the rabbits overnight in milk, and the next morning drain it off and place them in a huge pot which covered the top of the stove. She would gently simmer this for an hour or so, and as it became tender she would add roughly chopped vegetables from the garden, herbs and a little salt to season and simmer it all afternoon. When it was cooked through, she would add her dumplings. Mum and Dad called these 'doughboys', and they would rise to the top in huge fluffy balls. Sometimes Mum would make a sweet version with a little added sweetener, putting the dumplings in a pan of boiling water with a spoonful of honey and gently simmering them for about twenty minutes. With stewed fruit or a spoonful of honey this was a cheap and yet delicious pudding.

We seldom had puddings, but if Mum had some extra milk we had rice pudding. She would put the rice in a meat dish, add full-fat gold-top milk (Uncle Fred had two Jersey cows who gave enough to sell and give some away), as much sugar as she could spare as it was on ration and would sprinkle nutmeg on top. Lastly, she would add a small lump of margarine, or butter if she could get it. The meat dish would just fit into the oven, so Mum let the fire get low so that the pudding cooked slowly, and this sometimes took all afternoon. When it came out of the range, the cream on the milk somehow rose to the top, forming a rich creamy layer. We would have this for our supper with a spoonful of honey that Mum had been given. I have never tasted anything before or since like Mum's rice pudding.

When we had school meals, we usually had some sort of milk pudding but I hated them. One day, a greyish-brown sticky lump was plonked in front of me at lunchtime.

'What is it?' I asked truthfully.

The teacher glared at me.

'Haven't you ever seen rice pudding before?'

'Yes,' I replied, 'but my mother's don't look like that. My mother's tastes lovely and looks lovely!'

She looked at me in disbelief.

'I very much doubt that.'

I did not eat that rice pudding: even now, the very thought of it makes me feel ill.

I knew we were better off in many ways than the children I sat with in school. I took no notice at the time, but now I realise that many of them were terribly thin and emaciated. One or two children fainted regularly because of lack of food. One little girl in particular used to hide away at lunchtime. I did not know why at the time, but she probably did not have any lunch. Sometimes I didn't when my lunch was stolen, but that is not the same thing. We nearly always had something growing in the garden.

At least part of the day, when we were home from school, we were expected to help with the chores. There was no refusing. We just did as we were told. The job I hated most was picking up the potatoes; a dirty, back-breaking job. We never minded eating them, though, especially the tiny little ones which my mother just rinsed, cooked with a sprig of mint and tossed in a very little butter. As it was on ration, some people mixed their margarine and butter together to make it go further. Mum would never do this.

'I would rather have one delicious slice of bread and real butter than three of marge and butter,' she would say. She said the margarine ruined the butter, and it did. If Mum had some little potatoes left over, she would ask Granny for a bit of her beef dripping and then she would brown them in the dripping, scatter chopped parsley over the top and we would have this with maybe a fresh egg from our hens. If there was any to spare, Dad would have a bit of bacon with his. We all loved this meal, and my father would pat his stomach and say with a loud belch, 'That was fit for a king! Eat it all up or I'll 'ave it!'

This always made us laugh, as Dad was a frugal eater. Apart from his bread and butter, which he dipped in his breakfast cup of tea, he ate only one meal a day, saying that was enough for any man, and he always saved titbits for his ferrets.

We never had new bread. Mum said it would give us indigestion, but now I realise it was because a new loaf wouldn't go as far as a day-old one. But, on winter afternoons, a treat would be to sit in front of the glowing range making thick slices of toast with the brass toasting fork. By the time we were finished, we were well toasted ourselves. Then we would spread the toast with dripping and salt. I could not eat this now, but then it was a meal fit for royalty in our eyes.

The baker came in his horse-drawn van every morning. The smell, when he opened the flaps of the van, was heavenly. The bread and buns were still hot, and Dad would sometimes buy us a hot penny bun each if he had a few coppers to spare. I can still smell and taste them, yeasty and buttery, melting in the mouth. We could make these buns last for ages as we savoured every mouthful. One day he bought a huge crusty loaf for a treat. I thought I would just have a little nibble from the crust where it wouldn't be noticed. Then some from the other corner. And the little lump under the middle.

By the time Mum saw the loaf, most of the wonderful crust was gone, and only the doughy bits were left. What a sight! Dad laughed uncontrollably, but Mum was upset and angry. I knew I had done wrong, and felt guilty, but even getting walloped was almost worth it. I was never trusted with a new loaf again. Granny gave us one of her loaves as she had half a dozen loaves a day to feed my uncles. She had a bread hamper made of pine with leather hinges, and a big brass fastener on the front. It was big enough for a dozen loaves or more. It was my job to scrub this hamper every Saturday morning. If it had any crumbs left in the corners afterwards, I would have to do it all over again. It took ages, and I hated cleaning the brass fastener, but how I would love to own that hamper today!

Usually Mum gave us our supper outside. I liked to sit on the wagon steps to have mine. We had our main meal in the evening, usually a crust of bread and a tomato. Dad had the same, but with a slice of cold meat if there was any left over from Sunday. He used to have a dab of mustard with it, which I envied. It looked so delicious. I kept on and on at my Dad to give me a bit.

'No,' said Dad, 'you wouldn't like it.'

But I was convinced that I would love it. Finally, just to be left in peace Dad gave in, and passed me a small piece of bread with a dab of that lovely yellow stuff. At once I popped it into my mouth. Gasping and choking, tears running down my face, I managed to spit it out. Dad offered me a drink, holding it against my lips, but I pushed it away and ran as fast as I could to Mum. I couldn't trust Dad, at least for that moment.

'That,' said my mother, 'will teach you not to keep on asking for what's bad for you.'

I got over it in time, and Dad promised me a treat. I

looked forward to it until I found out that I had to weed the garden. The boys had made themselves scarce. They hated weeding as well. So I was left with tears of rage running down my burning cheeks until Dad said, 'Come on! I can hear the ice-cream van.'

I ran to the gate but Tiny, my dog, was there before me, head high, ears alert. Dad bought me the biggest ice cream on the van, and a small one each for himself and Tiny.

We three sat down on the grassy verge. The warm sun shone down on Dad, me and my lovely dog as we enjoyed our ice creams. All was quiet until suddenly I heard Dad choke. Quick as a flash, I turned to see him gasping as though in pain. I then realised he was trying hard not to laugh. I stared at him in quiet anger, daring him to laugh at me. It was too late. He doubled over, red in the face and trying so hard not to enrage me again, he spluttered and let out great bellows of laughter.

'Your face!' he bellowed hoarsely. 'You should have seen it!'

As I pictured it from his viewpoint I started to giggle, then laughed out loud as if I couldn't stop. Poor little Tiny pawed me anxiously, not knowing what was happening. Even the ice-cream man was tittering away as well – we had set him off too!

Later, exhausted with laughter, I saw my face in a mirror and realised why Dad had found me so amusing. Smeared with mustard, dirt, tears and a smidge of ice cream around my lips, I looked like 'nobody's child'.

*

I well remember the winter of 1947. I was aged about eight and a half. Snow fell relentlessly day after freezing day. Our caravan was always very warm and cosy, and the little range got so hot the small round covers on top of the stove glowed bright red. We had no guard around this stove, but we knew enough to keep well away from it. In spite of the fierce heat, ice formed on the inside of the windows as well as the outside, making pretty fern shapes on the cold glass.

I didn't have to fetch the milk when it was that cold; instead the older boys would leave us a couple of bottles when they got their own. One freezing morning I reached out to get it from the step and the milk had frozen solid in the bottles and had forced its way up through the neck, just like a lolly. The lids were stuck to the solid milk like jaunty little caps, and my brothers and I thought this very funny. Even the clothes on the line froze into strange shapes where the icy wind had blown them to and fro. Nothing could be dug up in the garden, either. I recall my father coming home one dark evening, tired and cold. He handed my mother a small sack.

'I did a job today fer one of the market gardeners,' he explained. 'They gave me this as payment.'

Mum opened the bag and revealed a shrivelled, yellowing cabbage, a handful of carrots, turnips, onions, swedes and something wrapped in greasy paper. It was half a sheep's head. He had worked nine or ten hours in the freezing wind, taking down old greenhouses for this paltry wage. He quickly divided it in half, and under my mother's shocked gaze, calmly walked out of the door.

'Where are you going with that, Eddy?'

'I'm just taking our mam her share.'

Mum could say nothing. We shared in good times, why should it be any different in bad? I remember that meal as if it were yesterday. Mum made a delicious stew with the sheep's head and vegetables. She gently cooked the meat until it was tender, and then added the veg and a few cloves of wild garlic. She had just enough flour and suet to make a few dumplings. Dad returned a while later with a loaf of slightly stale bread, but no matter: we all sat where we could get the most warmth from the stove while Mum toasted thick slices of the bread to eat with our bowls full of stew. For some time all was quiet, except for the sound of us eating and, 'Yummy, this is good!' mutters from all of us. Dad finished first and, leaning back in his chair, said, 'I couldn't have eat better at the Ritz!' As if he would know. Chrissy joined in.

'If I had more, I'd bust me belly!'

We all laughed, but Mum was very quiet. She knew that tomorrow would bring the same problems.

The winter continued for what seemed like for ever at the time. The snowdrifts reached to the tops of the hedges and when we went out, we couldn't tell if we were walking on the road or the tops of the bushes. I felt cold in spite of wearing several layers of clothing; mine and some of my brothers'! In an effort to keep warm while outside, I once put on all the jumpers and old coats I could manage. I could not lower my arms, and they stuck out from my sides at right angles to my body. Mum said I looked like a living scarecrow, which sent us all off in fits of laughter. We wondered when that winter would ever end, but it did and then there were floods to add to our misery.

Sometimes Dad did odd jobs for the farmers round about. One night he came home and told Mum that the farmer's wife had made thirty Christmas puddings and dozens of mince pies, and her table was stacked with chickens and turkeys. Dad was a proud man, but for our sakes he asked the farmer if he could spare anything for the children's Christmas dinner. Dad had done some extra work, as we were really hard up at the time. His wife handed him a scrawny old hen and a few cracked eggs. Dad wanted to refuse her scrag ends, but as the saying goes: beggars can't be choosers. Mum made the best of it as always, and we sat down to a chicken stew with fluffy dumplings, which we all enjoyed.

Several old people in the village died of the cold in 1947. There was a lot of illness, and most likely this was due to a lack of decent food. As is usually the case in wartime, people could get almost anything they wanted if they had the money. We managed fairly well because we grew our own food, but this had to feed about thirty people living on Granny's bit of land. Often visiting travellers would mean more mouths to feed, sometimes up to twelve more people. We had lots of vegetables, we all knew how to forage in the fields and hedgerows for nuts, berries and mushrooms and most of the men poached, which all helped our meals stretch.

Many people went hungry, though, while the land was full of rabbits, hares and sometimes a deer or two. We coped by using everything we had, eating everything we could buy or grow and never wasted as much as a tea leaf. Every drop of rainwater was collected and we used it to wash our hair in. Rainwater made our hair soft and silky, and any water left over after washing dishes or rinsing clothes watered Mum's little garden. I well know how it feels to have to be careful with every drop of water, and did not need to be told how precious it was. Even the youngest Gypsy child knew that it would mean a trip to the river if we needed another bucket filled.

One very cold day, we were all feeling hungry and my little brother asked Mum for a piece of bread and jam.

'I can't give you any, son. We'll have to wait for Daddy to come back. He might've been able to get some on the way home.'

'I'm hungry now,' he said sadly. Then his face brightened. 'Can I have a piece of toast, then? I don't mind toast.'

Lucky for us that we all had a sense of humour. We laughed and laughed as little Christopher sang, 'Toast, toast, give me some toast!'

He was too young to realise that toast was made from bread. We older ones never asked Mum for more than she could give, as we knew how sad she would get when she had to say no. That day, though, Dad had made enough money to buy some bread and a few groceries. We did not mind that the bread was a day old. Mum made toast and dripping, and it could not have tasted better if it had been roast chicken. Chris sat in front of the fire, his little mug in one hand and a piece of toast and the last of Mum's home-made jam in the other. He grinned at us with a rim of milk and jam around his mouth.

'Me likes toast!'

'Amen to that,' said my mother. 'It's just as well!'

Sometimes when times were very hard, that is all we had for days on end. Even dry toast was better than none. My brother Teddy was a great saver. He saved every penny he had ever been given. He was just a small boy of almost four when Mum was looking into her purse one day to see what money she had left. She tipped it into her lap: just a sixpenny bit and a few coppers was all she had. Her head dropped into her hands and we watched her weep silently in dismay. At once Teddy got up and fetched his money box and tipped it straight into her lap with the rest. We stared at him in wonder. We never saved anything, but spent our pennies as soon as we got them. It was a huge sacrifice for him to give his money away. Mum could hardly believe it, and looked into his angelic face with his blond curls and blue eyes.

'Thank you, Teddy,' she whispered. 'I will try and pay you back.'

Teddy smiled back at her and then, copying one of the gestures he had seen the men make when they were haggling, he spread his hands wide and, with a little shrug, spoke.

'That's all right, my dear,' he said gallantly. 'Any time will do.'

My mother laughed through her tears. She would never have taken Teddy's money, but she was desperate. That was the first time, but it was not the last.

Sometimes things would improve for a while, and Mum would buy us the things we needed. She would give Teddy his money back with a few pennies extra as 'interest', and then sometimes had to borrow it back again. Teddy bought a calf when he was nine years old. It was the runt of the herd, but he reared it until it was a fine cow and then took it to market and sold it for a good profit. He certainly deserved it, as he was a hard worker and knew how to use his money as well as save it.

Yes, my mother struggled so hard to keep us all fed and clothed, and with the help of our large extended family she managed. Not one of us had an ounce of fat to spare. My mother was very tiny and my father was strong and sinewy. At school we were weighed once or twice a year by the school doctor, who would prescribe orange juice, jars of malt and cod liver oil. My brother Nelson was prescribed the latter two delicacies, both of which he loathed. My mother made sure he had his dose every night before he went to bed, but it did not seem to make much difference to him as he was still very skinny.

Mum was called in to see the headmaster, and when she arrived he was waiting alongside the doctor. In front of the whole class, he proceeded to speak to my mother in a hectoring tone of voice.

'Why isn't this boy improving?' he boomed. 'He's far too thin. Is he being given his malt, cod liver oil and orange juice?'

My mother was shocked, more at his tone than the content of his speech.

'Yes, every night without fail!'

'Are you *sure*?'

'Yes, of course I'm sure.'

Nelson hated the stuff so much, she almost had to hold him down every night.

'The other children look well enough. You're sure they're not having it instead of this *poor thin boy*?'

Mum's amusement at this thought almost overcame her anger and she laughed in his face.

'Don't be foolish! They can't even bear the smell! To tell you the truth, I think it's this horrible stuff that's making him ill. By the time I give it to him, he's worked himself up into such a state that I almost take pity on him and let him off the dose!' But she added, 'I never have, though.'

The headmaster gave Mum a look of disgust.

'In future, he will be given his dose at school. We will make *sure* he gets it.'

Mum agreed to this, knowing what would happen when he was forced to take The Dreaded Dose. She was relieved she would not have to do it. She was worn out with it all, and to be spoken to like that in front of a classroom full of children who would, no doubt, go home and relate an embellished version to their parents, was the last straw.

The next morning, we waited with bated breath as one of the kinder teachers agreed to give Nelson his medicine. We waited as Nelson was taken into another room. Not a sound could be heard at first, but then we heard the teacher's voice. It was obvious that she was very cross, but not a sound from Nelson. That did not worry me. I knew what he was like with Mum. He never uttered a sound, but would sit with his teeth clamped tight.

Shortly, we heard the teacher speaking to the headmaster. She was gasping and saying, 'Never, never again!' She opened the classroom door and all eyes turned in her direction. Her hair hung in rat's tails around her face which was red and sweaty, and her smart blouse was plastered in the horrible malt and cod liver oil concoction. She was close to tears as our teacher turned to speak to her, and she flung her hands up in despair. Seconds later, in strolled my brother, his face hot and sticky and his front plastered with gunge. Some of the children held their noses as he took his seat. The fishy smell was awful, but Nelson sat at his desk looking very pleased with himself. The teacher looked at him and then at me.

'Take him home, Rosemary,' he sighed. 'Get him cleaned up.'

For once, Nelson did not mind being the centre of attention, and I almost expected him to take a bow. He grinned all the way home. Mum was not at all surprised to see him come home, and we did not go back to school that day. Mum had to wash his clothes as she did not have enough spare to give him clean ones.

We all hated The Dreaded Dose, but some of our schoolmates actually liked it. One child, whom I remember very well, used to bring cod liver oil and malt sandwiches to school for his lunch! No one would sit near him because of the terrible smell.

My mother never had any more problems from the school doctors, and Nelson never had malt and cod liver oil forced upon him ever again. We were all pleased about that. Nelson remained pale and thin, but even as a child could eat enough for two men and after would say to my mother, 'I'll put me plate in the cupboard, Mammy. You don't need to wash it cuz I've licked it clean!'

When the teachers thought we were starving and that we did not know what a good meal was, they were so wrong. Our hair, good teeth and complexions testified to that. I knew if I was hungry I shouldn't ask for more, as Mum didn't have it to give us. I learned later that she gave most of her food to us, often eating only a couple of slices of bread and a cup of cocoa a day. But one day we had a treat that I never forgot. She gave us some pink fish out of a small tin on a thick slice of bread and butter for our supper. I had never tasted anything so delicious in my life. For months I begged my mum for some of that pink fish, but there was no more to be had.

Years later I mentioned it to her, and she explained that it was the only tin of salmon she had managed to get during the war. It had been just enough for us four children. Mum said she would have loved a slice herself, but there hadn't been enough, and we ate it without a thought, as children do. If there wasn't enough to go around my mother often went without, but of course we children didn't know that at the time. My mother was really tiny and slim. From the back she looked like a very young girl. We never thought that in fact she was too skinny, and it never even entered my father's head that she was underweight. None of us had any fat on us. We just accepted her as she was.

One very cold day, Mum seemed very quiet. As she helped me do up my buttons, she suddenly stopped.

'Do these buttons up for Rosie, Eddy,' she asked my father. 'My hands feel strange.'

Dad quickly helped me with my buttons and then grabbed Mum's hands.

'Mary!' he gasped. 'You be shakin' like a leaf!'

'I'm a bit cold. Don't worry, I'll be all right when I've had a cup of tea.'

'Sit down, gel. I'll get a hot drink.'

Mum sat down thankfully, and Dad put the kettle on the range to boil.

'I'll get 'ee a bit o' toasted bread.'

'There's only just enough for the children,' she explained as he opened the food cupboard. He had no idea what a struggle Mum had to feed us. Mum, in common with many other women in those days, was too proud to admit that it was hard to manage week to week, and somehow thought it was their fault if the money would not last or there was not enough food to feed the family. Dad seemed shocked at what she had just said and quickly realised that she must be starving. I looked at my lovely mum. She was very pale and she tried to smile.

'Don't you worry,' she said, 'I'll soon be fine.'

She slowly stood up, smiling at us all, and before our terrified eyes she fell to the floor. I took one look at her and, thinking she was dead, I screamed and screamed. It seemed that everyone came running.

'Whatever is the matter?'

'Mammy's dead! Mammy's dead!' I whimpered.

Granfer took his whisky bottle out of his coat pocket and tried to force whisky into her mouth, but Mum's eyes just flickered for a moment.

I remember the village doctor was called; a very rare occurrence, as Granny usually 'cured' us. He looked very grave and told my distressed father that she was weak from lack of food, and was suffering from malnutrition. I have never forgotten him saying that big word. It sounded so terrible. My father felt so guilty, and sad that he had not noticed Mum was literally fading away. Apparently, all that Mum had eaten for months was two thin slices of bread and two or three cups of tea a day. Needless to say, we all watched that she had her fair share of food after that. My father, who was a frugal eater, almost forced her to eat, but she never got fat. Her health did improve, and she looked much better. I never forgot that terrible feeling of loss, though, and for a long time after I was afraid to leave my mother in case she died while I was not there.

When all the crops of wheat, hay, peas, beans, potatoes and everything green had been 'safely gathered in', we were told at school that it was a time of thanksgiving and we must give, out of our plenty, gifts to the poor. Every child was expected to bring something for the harvest table. We went home and told our parents, as did every other child in the school, and I have no doubt that there was many a look of consternation among them. I expect they wondered, as our family did, who were the poor we were expected to donate these gifts to? It must have been hard for some of the parents to find anything to give, as it was difficult enough to feed their own children.

Most of the children managed to bring something. The harvest gifts were laid out on a long trestle table around the centrepiece of a wonderful loaf of bread shaped like a wheat sheaf, baked and donated by the local baker. It smelled delicious, but after a few days looked a bit the worse for wear as someone or some*thing* had nibbled around the edges. Although I had history regarding nibbled new-baked bread, for once I was not guilty. It could have been mice. The rest of the gifts consisted of a few swedes, some battered cabbages, some leeks and garden veg. This had been arranged very artistically by the teachers and some of the children. In between the vegetables were some rusty tins of baked beans and other sundry foods that had very obviously been lurking in the backs of cupboards for some time.

Draped across this display was a large bunch of black grapes, again donated by a local grocer. We had never seen anything like these luscious grapes; they fairly made our mouths water! It seems hard to believe that the teachers could display fruits like these before children who were so deprived of such natural foods, and expect them to remain untouched. Suffice to say that by the end of the first day, the bunch of grapes was half its original size. No one asked who the guilty party was, and the straggly stalks were removed and another bunch donated to replace it.

On the day of the harvest festival the vicar came to

tell all of us poor, underfed, barely clothed children how blessed we were to live in the village, where everyone had enough wordly goods. I thought he must have mistaken us for someone else. I do not know who received the bounty of our gifts, or if they would even have wanted any of it. Most of us had cabbages and swedes for the asking, having been encouraged to 'dig for victory' over the past few years. Surely no one would have welcomed the rusty tins. But we *were* blessed to live near our pretty village, and the wonderful green countryside surrounding us.

After the vicar's sermon, the room was cleared and a few of the favoured parents were ushered in and seated in the few small chairs around the room. Needless to say, none of the Gypsy parents were invited, but I am sure they were not very sorry about this.

We all filed in wearing our tatty black daps and anything that our parents could find to dress us in. The boys looked gawky, their skinny knees showing above socks sliding down to their ankles. We all looked less than smart because one little girl was wearing a blue satin dress that must have belonged to a taller and much larger child. To add to this glory, her mother had dressed her hair with many odd bits of ribbon, and finished off her creation with a pair of ladies' silver sandals, also far too big for her.

At the teacher's instructions, we all formed a ring and she clapped her hands for attention.

'Now we are pleased to present a display of country dancing!' she announced with a flourish. 'Afterwards, there will be a collection for a local children's charity and I'm *sure* you will all give generously. Light refreshments will be provided.'

She nodded to the pianist in the corner of the hall and the music began. We did not. After a few false starts we managed to get going and began skipping around in one direction. The girl in the blue satin dress tripped over the hem, and when we had to stop and kick our legs up, her silver sandal flew off her tiny foot and landed in front of the audience. Right on cue, the boys deliberately kicked off their daps and the audience became hysterical. Blue Satin Dress, who had retrieved the sandal, lost it on the next kick and it flew into the lap of a huge man who immediately picked it up and dropped on one knee before the lady next to him and pretended to be Prince Charming. The whole performance came to a raucous end and Prince Charming took a bow.

'That was the best laugh I've ever had!' he said. I do not remember if they had a collection, but a good time was had by all, and we went home smiling and gave thanks for a happy day.

Pets and Other Animals

hen I first started noticing things and inter-
acting with the animals, which I saw daily,
it was the dogs I loved best of all. They were
all gentle with me and put up with the constant inter-
ference of a small child. They let me climb on their
backs and pull their ears and tails, and they shared every
treat. My own dog, Tiny, a Welsh border collie, came
first in my affections. She was born on the same day that
I was. When she was six weeks old, Dad brought her
home for me.

From that day on she was my friend and protector. No
one would dare raise their voice to me, let alone their
hand, in my presence, while Tiny was around. She
would run around me in circles, growling and barking
and generally raising mayhem. She would have laid
down her life for me, so loyal was she. In turn, I loved
and cared for her. She knew everything about me, and
never told a soul. She saw me off to school, and was
there waiting at the gate when I returned. I shared all
my treats with her whenever I had any, but her favourite
was ice cream.

We often shared a biscuit, bite for bite, to the horror of

my mother, but I never came to any harm. We were used to each other's germs. Dad said that the dog was more at risk than I was.

Tiny was there when I was very young indeed, and I was given a really pretty dress. Young as I was, I can still see it in my mind's eye. It was made of soft velvety material with a frill on the hem and little blue flowers on the collar. Mum got ready as well, and said we would be going out later. First, she picked up a little box.

'Come on, Rosie, I want to take a photograph of you in your new frock.'

She lifted me down the wagon steps and stood me next to Tiny. I held onto her collar and offered her a bite of my apple. Mum pointed the camera just as Uncle Alfie, dressed in his oily work clothes and with a dirty face, stepped into view.

When the photo was printed, there I was offering my apple to my Uncle Alfie in all his oily glory. I have the photo still, minus Alfie, as Mum had cut him out of the picture.

'He ruined that photo!' she said, snipping him off.

Mum always did this to photos, cut off the bit she did not like. The minute after the photo had been taken, I had lifted up my arms to be picked up and, before Mum could intervene, Uncle Alfie had obliged and given me a hug in my lovely white dress. Mum said, much later, that she wished she had taken a photo of me after with the oily splodges over my cheeks and my dress covered in oil. The dress was never the same, as the marks never came out and I cannot remember ever wearing it again.

*

Tiny always knew when the ice-cream van would come, long before we heard his bell, and would wait, tail wagging, by the gate. If Dad bought us an ice cream, Tiny would have one as well. She lay with the cone between her paws, licking it as elegantly as any lady. Often the ice-cream man would give her a cone just for the pleasure of watching her eat it.

One horrible day, the van drove off just as Tiny was coming in and Tiny flew under the wheels. The poor man was so distraught and burst into rapid Italian, gripping his head in his hands, the tears running down his cheeks. In spite of my own grief, we managed to calm him down. My father walked slowly to the prone little furry body and bent down. He looked up as we waited, in dread of his words. He shook his head. Tiny was gone. He told me to go inside while he sorted things out. He got a spade and sadly began digging a grave for poor Tiny at the bottom of the garden. I watched, my nose pressed to the glass of the trailer window as he finished, stood up and beckoned to me. He knew I would want to be there when he buried her.

We walked back to the gate together, not speaking a word. When we got to where she lay, she suddenly shook her head, leaped up and staggered towards us on wobbly legs! My joy knew no bounds. I gathered her up in my arms and let her lick my face all over. We lost no time in telling the dear ice-cream man, who had sat back in his van, his head still in his hands. He then burst into tears of joy. Tiny always had a free ice cream after that.

When she had pups, I invited a boy who lived further up the road to come and see them.

'Do you like my dog?' I asked.

'She's not a dog, she's a bitch,' he informed me. I was furious and turned on him with a hefty thump.

'Don't you call my dog a bitch!' I screamed. Tearfully, I ran to my father to tell him what he had said. He had to have a drink of water before he could stop laughing at my indignant, tear-stained face.

She was always having pups. Dad locked her away in a shed at times, but she often got out. Not knowing why she was locked in, I would let her out myself, and some time later we had the joy of five or six pups to play with. They were all so gorgeous that we had no trouble finding them new homes, but we never wanted them to go and shed tears over the loss of each one, our pleadings falling on deaf ears.

She had one of her litters under the air-raid shelter. Dad said to leave her in peace. I did try, but I just *had* to have a little peek. The nearest way was over the murky ditch that ran along the back of our caravan. It was full of duckweed and rubbish, but there was no way over now. Then I saw an old oil drum half submerged. I reasoned that if it was half sunk, it was safe enough. I didn't realise that it was empty and would tip over as soon as I stepped on it. Sure enough, as soon as I placed one foot upon it, it suddenly lurched forward, rolling and tipping me head first into the filthy shallow water.

I managed to grasp an overhanging branch and drag myself out. Appalled by the stink and feel of my slimy, sopping clothes I ran screaming through the yard. My

Uncle Tom had just come home and, seeing my appearance, roared with laughter. My mother ran down the steps and was horrified at the sight of me, and just stood there wondering what to do. Uncle Tom took pity on us both, and, telling me to stand over the wash-house runaway, he proceeded to hose me down. Fortunately it was summer, so the water didn't feel quite so cold. I was relieved just to have the thick slime washed off me. So why, then, did I do almost the same just a few days later?

My youngest brother Christopher had an old three-wheeled bike someone had given him. I decided to show him a few tricks to impress him, as older siblings do. So I showed off for a while, until suddenly the bike veered uncontrollably towards the same ditch.

So there was I, stinking, wet and being hosed down yet again. That was my last warning, though, as my father said that next time I would be left to dry out. See how I would like that! I never did it again.

Tiny died when she was fourteen, as I was, and took my childhood with her. I missed her so much. She taught me the meaning of loyalty and caring. She was far more than a dog. She was a friend.

We were usually good when we played in the fields, but looking back I realise we had no sense of the land not belonging to all and sundry. The fields round about us were our playground. I knew very well, though, that when any damage was done, it was the Gypsies who were blamed, and my parents and my uncles paid compensation, sometimes unfairly. This was agreed between our families and the farmers who usually rubbed along well together and who gave us our milk still warm from the cows every morning. There was one farmer, however, who tried to cause as much trouble for us as he could.

One day when all the men were away, I was sitting on the steps of one of the wagons when I noticed him trying to open the five-bar gate to our yard. He had his bull with him, and instinctively I knew what he intended to do. I stood up and screamed at the top of my voice, whereupon he hurriedly retreated. My aunts and mother came out instantly.

'What on earth's the matter, child?' they asked.

'It was the bad man – he was going to let his bull loose in our yard!' I cried.

My mother dashed out and confronted him, bull and all, but he denied coming anywhere near the gate. Mum had to let it go, and said she believed him. But to this day I know he intended to let his bull loose in our yard. I think my mother knew it too, but there was nothing she could do. That bull could have caused a lot of damage, or even killed one of us. But we were only Gypsies. Who would have cared? I had nightmares for a long time after that, his evil face as he tried to unfasten the gate a vision that has stayed with me until this day. But his type was a rarity, thank goodness.

Behind our camp were fields full of wheat and hay, or other crops. As children, we loved to watch the wheat being cut and tied by hand into sheaves and then left to dry in the sun. When they brought the threshers and combined harvesters in, the air was filled with noise and dust as they did the work of many men. The men and women who worked during the harvest would get browner by the hour as they worked in the hot sun. They would stop when the sun got high and sit in the shade of the carts or under the hedges, eating bread and cheese and swilling back stone bottles of cider.

It was a wonderful time of year, so much going on, everyone busy as bees, appearing tired but happy. Little did we know that some of the labourers were just existing in the midst of plenty. The farmers all cried poverty, but I never saw a poor one. They all looked fat and jolly to me. But I loved the haymaking best of all, when the laden farm carts would trundle down the narrow lanes at dusk. In the morning, the hedgerows would have swathes of hay caught on the twigs from the hay carts brushing past. The hay would then be formed into hayricks, some of which were works of art. Sometimes these would catch fire due to overheating. This would be a tragedy to the farmer, as he would have lost all his winter feed and would have to buy it for his animals.

We loved to play on the hayricks, little realising that we were taking our lives in our hands when we jumped from the top or tunnelled inside. None of us was ever harmed, thankfully, although we got a good hiding when we were found out. It never stopped us, though.

I was walking back from the farm one day, when I saw my cousin Paul playing on one of the hayricks.

'Hey! Come and see what I've done!' he yelled, beckoning to me from the top. I eyed him warily. He was twice my size and strong, and I had come off worse from some of his tricks before. My curiosity got the better of my common sense, so I pushed open the gate and walked across the field towards him.

'Look!' he said. He had made a tunnel through the hayrick on all four sides, that ran into the centre.

'Watch me!' he commanded. 'I'll tunnel right through to the other side. Go round and watch me come out!'

He performed this feat several times, coming out of a different entrance each time. I gazed at him in admiration. He stood in front of me, handsome and glowing, with wisps of straw sticking out of his ears and hair.

'Go on,' he coaxed, 'you have a go!'

I looked longingly at the hayrick. Paul made it seem so much fun, but something stopped me. I didn't trust him. He could charm the birds off the trees, but he had caught me out once too often.

'No, I don't want to.'

'You're a scaredy cat!'

'No, I'm not!'

'Well, why not have a go, then? It's fun!'

I could see it was fun, and I wanted to try it out so badly. Well, I thought, why not have a go? What could hurt me?

'All right, then,' I agreed. 'Just once.'

I thought I saw a sly grin cross his face, and I nearly turned back.

'Come on, Rosie,' he said, catching hold of my arm and gently tugging me forward. 'I'll walk home with you afterwards.'

Almost against my will, I knelt down and entered the sweet-smelling tunnel. I could see the light from the opposite side. I would soon be out, I thought. As I

212

neared the light, Paul stuffed the hay back in, preventing my escape. My heart leaped with fear, and I turned awkwardly in the tiny space to go back the other way, but he did the same at this other exit. I knew he was not going to let me out, and I was sobbing with terror. He blocked up the other two passages, just as I had thought he would. I was now breathing in straw and dust, and felt almost unconscious with the heat. When he had had his fun, he relented and pulled me out. It was several minutes before I could breathe properly again. My nose was running and the tears and snot stuck my hair to my face. Then I saw Paul, watching me fearfully from the gate.

Getting to my feet, I started to scream. I screamed and cried all the way home; I could not stop. My father heard me screaming all the way down the road and came out immediately. I could not even tell him what had happened, I was so hysterical. Granny came out into the yard, then went to fetch a glass of water. She threw it in my face. It was not pleasant, but it did the trick. Gasping and choking, I told all that had gathered around me what had happened. At first, they could not see what all the fuss was about, but when my parents went to find the milk I had left behind and saw what Paul had done to the hayrick, they were shocked and scared. Dad went back to find Paul, but he was nowhere to be seen, which was probably just as well because I think Dad would have given him a taste of his own medicine.

Even now, I have to be where I can see my way out, and I hate anything over my face. Paul was only a little older than me, and I do not think he meant me any real harm, but I know I could have died that day.

Paul was a constant source of irritation to me. I never knew how to take him. Sometimes when I was playing in the yard I would hear his loud voice shouting, 'Rose! Rose!' On looking up to see what he wanted, he would walk on, completely ignoring me, and carry on singing, 'Rose, Rose, I love you, Chinese Romeo sing!' as though that was his only intention, and I was left looking and feeling foolish. But that was Paul; he had to win.

Although he was only a month older than me he was much bigger and he crowed the whole time that he was 'a year older', never missing an opportunity to remind me. He was always trying to get the better of me, and if I had something he wanted, he would not rest until he had it for himself.

As usual, we were both walking back from the farm with the milk cans. It was a lovely sunny day, and the lane was dry for a change. I saw a black cloaked figure gliding towards us, and we both stopped in our tracks. As the figure approached, we could see it was a nun on a 'sit up and beg' bicycle. She stopped when she drew alongside us, got off the bike and waited for us to approach her. For some reason, even unknown to myself, I was terrified of nuns. We saw quite a few of them in the village in their black and white habits, and they always looked stern and bad-tempered. My mother told me they were 'only ladies', and some were very kind. She said they were called 'sisters of mercy' and did a lot of nursing, helping those who were poor and needy. Her explanation made no difference; I was still scared of them. As we got nearer, she smiled at me.

'Hello, dear. I wonder if you would mind holding my bike for me while I pick some flowers?' She nodded towards some wild yellow irises growing along the edge of the ditch. I was too scared to say no, so I silently took the handlebars and stood shaking while she collected her bouquet. Paul began making faces at me behind her back, and laughed silently. I grimaced in return, but I was trembling like a leaf. The nun came back and placed a large bunch of yellow blooms into the basket on the front of the bike, and then slid her hand into her robe. She rummaged about for a bit and drew out a shiny coin.

'Thank you, my dear,' she said in a beautiful voice. 'You are most kind. Tell your mummy what a good child she has!'

Placing a sixpence into my hand, she gave a little wave and rode off. Paul started laughing at me, and putting on a silly voice said, 'Tell your mummy what a *wonderful* child she has!' For once, I ignored him. His expression turned serious.

'You'd best give me that money to look after, Rosie. She's prob'ly p'isened it. Give it me an' I'll throw it away so yer won't be hurted.'

He held out his hand. For once, I was not taken in by him.

'No, Paul,' I said firmly. 'If I gives it you, *you* might be hurted.'

I picked up my milk can and began walking back. He then tried every ploy he could to wrest the sixpence from my possession, but I reasoned that if I had been brave enough to hold the nun's bike, then the sixpence would do me no harm. When I told my mother about the nun and gave her my sixpence, she smiled.

'Well done for not letting Paul have it. Now you can see that nuns are only ladies dressed up, and nothing to be afraid of.'

I was not wholly cured, and still continued to be nervous of them, avoiding them whenever I could. I told Mum that the nun had said that I was 'a good child, and my mummy must be proud of me because I was most kind'. This sent my mother into fits of laughter because I recounted the tale in the nun's voice.

'If you could keep speaking like that, Rosie,' she said, 'it would take you a long way!'

I tried it for a while, until Granny looked at me strangely and asked if I had 'a plum in me mouth'. So that was the end of that. I did see the nun several times after that, always on her bike, but I would start to walk very fast, as though I was on an urgent errand. I no longer feared her, but I was taking no chances. It was Paul who had to be watched. He never stopped his tricks, and although he never did any real harm, we came close to it.

One day he brought home some strange round objects. He put one on the ground and pretended to hit it with a hammer. I watched him for a bit, and he ignored me at first.

'You can't have a go,' he said, straightening up. At once I was determined to have a go, but feigned indifference.

'I don't want to. It looks silly.'

He eyed me for a minute.

'All right. You can try. But don't tell nobody else.'

'No,' I said, 'I don't think I will.'

He bent as though to pick up the piece of metal.

'Oh, all right,' I said quickly. 'What must I do?'

'Just hit it hard.'

I banged away with the hammer ineffectually. Paul sighed.

'Give it yer!'

I handed him the metal object and he threw it at the solid fence by the wash house, whereupon it exploded with a loud bang and a flash of light. I discovered later that it was a fog signal that, when placed on the railway lines, would explode when the trains ran over them. If it had exploded while I was bent over it, the consequences could have been disastrous. Gladly, my puny strength was not enough.

The loud bang caused my father to come out to see what had happened. He immediately realised what it was and made a grab for Paul, shaking him until Paul begged him to stop. Dad did stop, and put his face into Paul's.

''Ee be always frightenin' our Rosie! She be half yer size!'

For a moment, Dad looked as though he was wondering what to do next. He turned to me.

'Rosie, come yer an' give 'im a punch. 'E might leave 'ee alone in future!'

I did not want to hit Paul. He looked very sorry for himself, but Dad was so angry. I lifted up my little hand to give him a tap but he flinched at the wrong moment and I just caught him on the nose. At once it poured with blood. I was terrified, and Dad let go of him immediately. He ran yelling to his mother. I did not know what he told her, but after all, he could hardly tell her that a little girl half his size had given him a bloody nose, could he? He hardly ever bullied me after that, so perhaps Dad was right after all.

My cousin Johnny absolutely adored all animals. He tried to train his little animals to perform all sorts of tricks, and many times he succeeded. He it was who showed me all the wild birds' nests, when they had laid their eggs. He told me never to steal their eggs and he never did either, but when they hatched he took an avid interest in their lives until they had all flown the nest. He adopted a young jackdaw whom he named Jack, and who always followed him to school, flying from tree to tree all the way there. While Johnny was in class, Jack perched on the blacksmith's roof and waited for Johnny until it was time to go home. If he had stayed on the blacksmith's roof, no one would have minded, but when Jack grew bored he made forays through the school-house's open bedroom windows, causing havoc and leaving droppings everywhere. This had to stop. Mr and Mrs Hendon, the school caretaker and his wife, who lived in the schoolhouse, complained to the headmaster. In turn, a note came from him to Miss Farr. Johnny was told to leave his bird at home or he would be in *big trouble*.

'That bird has caused too much trouble, John. It has to stop *at once*!'

Johnny stood up and faced his teacher. His hair stuck up wildly, his cheeks were rosy red. Huge tears welled up in his eyes.

'I can't leave 'im 'ome, Miss!' he said through his tears. ''E follers me. 'E follers me everywhere I goes!'

Johnny heaved a great sob.

''E loves me, yer see, Miss. 'E wants to be wiv me 'cos 'e loves me.'

Miss Farr was bemused. She looked at this little boy, who at times was the bane of her life and – surely – that was a tear in her own eye?

'Oh, Johnny,' she sighed, 'oh, Johnny.'

That was how we all felt about him. What could you do with a boy who loved all of nature as he did? Jack continued in this way for a long time after, until he finally met a natural end, but he was only the first in a long line of 'Jacks' who loved and 'follered' Johnny everywhere he went.

I used to fetch our milk in a white enamelled milk can. It was light enough going to the farm, but as heavy as lead when returning home full of creamy milk. I enjoyed going to the farm, though, as I could play with the lambs that were being bottle-fed, but as soon as they were big enough they joined the flock and another would take its place.

Sometimes Johnny fetched his mum's milk at the same time, and we would stroll along together. He knew where all the birds' nests were, and trusted me enough to show me. I loved to see the baby birds, beaks wide open, waiting for their mother to come back and feed them.

*

Johnny had a little pony, a strawberry roan, and she was his pride and joy. He used to let me ride her bareback sometimes. Many a roll in the mud I had before I finally mastered the art. We used to go and round up the cows in the farmer's field, until they stopped giving milk and we got a good hiding.

Before Johnny had this pony, he tried to ride Granfer's Billy Pony. We used to tether Billy on the wide green grassy verge that ran in front of the camp. The road adjacent was almost empty of traffic in those days, so it was quite safe to do this. A water-filled ditch ran the whole length on the inside of the verge. My father often warned Johnny not to try to mount Billy, as he was only used to pulling the cart. He persisted, until one day Billy had had enough. We heard shouting.

'Help! Help – Uncle Eddy!'

Waiting for him to turn his back, Billy had grabbed Johnny by the seat of his pants, given him a hefty shake, turned his head and dropped him in the ditch. Leaving our Johnny spitting up duckweed, Billy tossed his head and went back to his grazing.

My father, helpless with laughter, lifted him out of the ditch. Johnny ran home sobbing, and we didn't see him for some days. His dad told us that Johnny had teeth marks and a huge black bruise on his backside. We asked to see it, but he wouldn't show us.

After that, he crossed over to the other side of the road when he saw Billy. But when Billy died some years later, he grieved more than all of us. Months later, he came crying to Granfer. His pony had cut his leg on a piece of wire, and blood was pouring from the wound. He led the animal to Granfer.

'Make him well, Granfer,' he pleaded. Granfer took care of him and the horse lived to a ripe old age.

We were brought up surrounded by animals of all sorts, the edible and the inedible. We had cats and dogs, chickens, goats, cows and ponies, also a pet pig we called Sam. We hid balls in the straw for Sam to find and he would come when we called. When he went for bacon, we were sad for a time, but we knew it had to be done and ate the bacon with a sense of detachment. I never tired of looking at the piglets. We only had one pig, but Uncle Fred had several. We liked to see them feed.

'This is their dinner,' Uncle Fred would say, 'and they're having rhubarb and custard for after.'

Well, I thought, fancy a pig having pudding. We never did. I don't know why I believed it. Sometimes he let us hold a baby piglet. It was a lovely feeling, holding a pink, warm, squirmy piglet in my arms.

We made pets of them all, and then when they were on our plates, ate them thankfully. My father reared chickens that he would sell at Christmas. He always bred one especially for us, an extra-large one. One year we had a fine cockerel, a real beauty. We kept all our titbits for him and he got fatter and fatter. He hated us all, but the one he hated most of all was my beautiful little brother Teddy. Everyone loved him, with his blond hair and big blue eyes, except this mad bird. We never let Teddy near him, but one day he saw his chance and flew at poor

Teddy, knocking him to the ground and trying to peck his eyes out. We screamed and screamed. Thankfully, my father heard us and came running. Enraged at what he saw, he grabbed the bird by the throat, wrung its neck and threw it as far as he could. Teddy was safe, although he didn't cry. He was probably in shock. We ate the bird for Sunday dinner and enjoyed every mouthful. My father was always careful about what sort of birds he bought after that, and Teddy gave them a wide berth.

We knew that all animals served a purpose, and had to be sold or eaten. We had our dogs and cats to lavish our affection on, and we treated them all with respect. Some people think that Gypsy horses are ill treated. I only know that my family would have fed them before they fed themselves.

Finally, when Billy Pony was dying, my granfer sat by him all day stroking his head until Billy closed his eyes for the last time. Then he quietly walked away. He wouldn't let him be taken to the knacker's yard. He hired a digger so that Billy could be buried in his favourite spot in the field, to become part of the land he had grazed and galloped on for so many years. A fitting and dignified end for that dear old horse.

Pride, Prejudice and the Kindness of Strangers

hen I was about ten, it was time for Teddy to start school. He was four years old, and my mother was more than a little concerned as to how he would cope with day-to-day school life. Teddy was happy enough. He thought he would be treated the same as he was at home, that was, in our eyes, well and truly spoiled. He was still really just a baby . . . We decided to tutor him in the ways of school.

'What will you do if you want to go wee-wee, Teddy?'

He gave a big grin.

'Want potty, Teacher!'

'No, no. You put yer 'and up and say, "Please, Teacher, can I go to the lavatory?"'

He grinned again, and tried to repeat what we had suggested. After a few tries he got it right and we moved on.

'What do you have to do, Teddy, if you have to speak to the teacher and she's already speaking to someone else?'

'Teacher, Teacher, Teddy wants to say somefing!'

'No, Teddy, you say, "'Scuse me, Teacher," and the teacher will say, "What do you want, Teddy?" Then what will you say, Teddy?' I prompted. After a little thought and much screwing up of his baby-blue eyes, he said, 'I don't know, Teacher, I'se forgetted.'

We spent some days teaching Teddy what to say in different situations, until we thought he would be all right. Everybody loved our Teddy, so surely the teachers would as well. That is why we were all stunned when we discovered, at the end of a school day, that our much loved baby brother had been caned on both hands by the bully of a headmaster. What heinous crime had he committed, deserving of such punishment? He had put his elbows on the dinner table. What an evil thing to do to a small boy who was still really a baby! A child who did not know he should not put his elbows on the table, because he had never eaten at a table. We always ate our food on our laps in the wagon.

I was in another class, and we had our school meals at different sittings. I knew nothing of Teddy's caning until we got off the school bus and he held out his hands to show me the welts. I know for a fact that, had it been done in front of me, I would somehow have prevented it. My mother and father were very upset for Teddy, as were we all, but corporal punishment was unquestionably allowed in those days, and few thought it was wrong. We must be thankful that this does not happen now but if it is wrong now, it was wrong then.

Violet and I, and sometimes some of our other cousins, would congregate at the end of the lane which led to the fields and orchards. We would spend hours picking flowers and fruit from the hedgerows. When we ventured into the village, we seldom mixed with the *gadje* girls. We were happier on our own. One or two of the girls would mock our speech, and we would use lots of Romany words just to puzzle and annoy them. They often tried to find out what they meant, as did the teachers. I might have told them had I been alone, but I preferred their annoyance to Violet's wrath. These girls bullied us, which I hated, but Violet just ignored them as though they were invisible, which they hated in turn.

Our way of speaking was obviously different, and became apparent in different ways. In Bible class one day, we were told the story of Lot's wife. Our teacher ended the story with the emphatic conclusion: '. . . and Lot's wife became a pillar of salt!' Confused, Violet asked, 'A piller, like what you lays yer 'ead on, Miss?'

Violet shared a secret with me, about one of the teachers. When Violet's mother had been young, one of our teacher's husbands had tried to make a date with her, he also being single at the time. This was absolutely true. Violet's mother was very attractive, even to our eyes, and had been more so when she was younger. To our dismay, one of the girls overheard and ran to repeat this blasphemy to the teacher concerned. We were summoned to her at once. Crimson with restrained anger, she demanded that Violet repeat what she had said. The colour drained from Violet's face as she innocently repeated what she knew to be true. As I stood beside her, I could not take my eyes off our teacher's eyes as she shook with rage. Her anger knew no bounds as she spat out the allegation inches from Violet's face.

'Liar! My husband wouldn't go near a *Gypsy*!'

Looking at her, and seeing how ugly she looked at that moment, I thought it no surprise that he had wanted to take out my beautiful aunt. With her hands clenched behind her, Violet dared to repeat that she was telling the truth. I have never admired her more than when she faced this madwoman, and would not back down. She was caned twice on each hand as hard as was possible. Blue welts came up on her palms, but she never shed a tear. There was nothing I could do but stay close to her in wordless sympathy. If the teacher had ignored what a little girl had said, she would have saved herself from such an ignominious situation. Violet had come out of it with more dignity than she. But that is what some thought of Gypsies. Liars, dirty, cheats and more. I can only say that they were wrong about many things.

We went home and never told anyone else about it, knowing that it would only cause more trouble. I did wonder, though, much later, how the teacher's husband fared that evening on her return.

During our lessons, we could hear the other class having theirs through the partition. A male teacher took this class, and many of us dreaded the day when it would be our turn on the other side. He was not a good teacher, we thought. He seldom kept to the subject he was supposed to be teaching, and part of the way through he would reminisce about his exploits on Salisbury Plain during the war. We were quite impressed, knowing no better; in fact, it was far more interesting than his subjects, history and geography, which we found so dull. He was nothing but a bully, however. In his class were a brother and sister, who were almost as wide as they were tall. They both suffered dreadfully at his hands as day after day he called them unkind names. Of course, they sat quietly, not saying a word.

The term was drawing to an end, and the days got hotter and hotter. We were all on edge, and were not allowed to open the doors or windows. I sat there sweltering, longing for home time. The droning voice from behind the partition stopped and the room went very quiet. The partition hid what was going on, but there was an atmosphere of expectation. Suddenly, someone roared like a raging animal. There was a loud crash and then a scream. The partition began to sway, and part of it fell to the floor, exposing the scene beyond. As we all watched, open-mouthed, we saw the huge boy pick up the man who had been making his life a misery for so long, and throw him right over a row of desks. He hit the wall and slid down it into a silent heap on the floor. The boy instantly ran out of the room, out of the school, and the class was quickly ushered out and onto the school bus. The next day at school the teacher was at his desk on the other side of the partition, and his violent pupil was in his usual seat. All was calm, as if nothing had happened. After that, the teacher kept his taunts to himself, which was better for all of us.

My mother rarely made cakes, but once, for my birthday, she did. It was not easy, as our little range had no heat controls, so Mum just had to guess. She had saved her butter and sugar ration for weeks. She had eggs from our hens, and she borrowed flour from Granny. She got the fire in the range going, and brought the oven to what she guessed was the right temperature. I watched as she creamed and mixed everything up. It looked very good, even before it was cooked. She put the mixture into two sponge-cake tins and carefully slid them into the hot oven, giving me the bowl to scrape clean while she sat down to watch. I was right – it was delicious, even uncooked! Mum waited until she guessed the cake was ready, and took it out of the oven. It looked very nice and golden-brown. One of them sank just a bit.

'Don't worry, I'll make it look so nice, you won't notice it.'

Next she made some icing, and coloured some of it pink with some cochineal and spread some of her home-made strawberry jam in the middle. It was full of whole strawberries, and she gave me one to try. Straight away I wanted another, but she told me not to be greedy. Then she placed the top layer on carefully and iced it with the pink and white icing. When she put some little jelly sweets around the edge, the cake was finished. I gazed at this beautiful creation in amazement.

'It's lovely – no, it's more than lovely,' I breathed. 'I want to show everyone my cake!'

So I did. My brothers and I had a slice, and even Dad had a piece. He pronounced it as good as shop-bought. Mum laughed.

'If I could have got one in a shop, I would have done!'

'Yours is much better than shop cake!' I said, loyally. There was one more thing I wanted to do, and that was to take a slice of my birthday cake to my teacher, as I had often seen the other children do. They always ate it with their morning cup of tea.

The next day I took the little slice of cake, which my mother had wrapped in a pretty piece of tissue paper, and proudly offered it to my teacher. She took it and scrutinised it for a few seconds.

'Did your mother buy this cake?'

'Oh, no, Miss, she made it all by herself!'

She glanced at me and put the piece of cake on the corner of her desk.

'Well, Rosemary, tell your mother that it was very kind of her to think of me, and that I will enjoy eating it.'

I was pleased enough to hear this, and I knew Mum would be pleased as well.

'My mum worked hard to make that cake. We all liked it, even my dad.' She gave me a wintry smile.

'I'm glad to hear it. Now go and sit down.'

I was so happy to be able to give her a piece of cake, as the other girls did. I knew she would enjoy it with her cup of tea, but when break came, she left it on her desk. Perhaps she was not hungry, I thought. Later that morning, however, it was gone. I was glad, and thought maybe that she had eaten it later. I did not think of it again until the afternoon, when I was sent to get a tea towel from the line in the school garden. My eye was caught by a small piece of pink and white icing on the grass. It was the remains of my slice of cake. Instantly I knew that, rather than eat anything a Gypsy had touched, she had fed the birds with it. I was upset when I thought of the hard work it was for my mother to make me that cake, and the pleasure she and I had taken in giving it to my teacher. I was bitterly angry, but when Mum asked me if the teacher had enjoyed it, I told a barefaced lie and said she had said thank you, she enjoyed the cake very much. Mum looked pleased and happy. I could never have told her the truth; it would only have hurt her.

Oddly enough, some of these same teachers were not above asking for favours from our Gypsy parents. They expected to have their logs delivered cheaper than anyone else, and were under the misapprehension that they were getting a bargain. A price would be quoted much higher than usual, and then 'lowered' substantially, much to their delight. Then they would boast to their friends about it, not knowing they were paying far more than anyone else. They were not above accepting the odd rabbit or hare either, sometimes even a pheasant of dubious origin, haggling over the price, and yet they had the nerve to call us thieves. We always felt that anything running wild, even the pheasants, were free and God's bounty, and so could not understand why they called us thieves.

Although my father mostly dealt in scrap metal, he sometimes bought gold and silver and unusual bits and pieces if he thought he could sell them on for a profit. Most Gypsy men and women wear their savings on their person in the form of jewellery. They had no trust in banks, so they dealt in cash or horses and put their money into valuables, usually gold. My mother wore no jewellery, except her twenty-two-carat gold wedding ring, which I wear now. Besides, we had no spare money to waste on gold jewellery, as we needed it to live from day to day.

One year, however, he bought several gold sovereigns, and when I came home from school he showed me these beautiful gold coins. I held them in my palms, admiring them, until Dad took them back, all except one.

'That one is yours,' he said, smiling.

I was so happy to possess one of these lovely things (never having owned such riches before) that foolishly, without my parents' knowledge, I took my coin to school to show the other children. After, I hid it in a corner of my desk. At the end of the school day, when I went to get it, it was not there. I felt sick. I burst into tears. The teacher asked me what the matter was. When I told him, he was very angry.

'You should not have brought it to school in the first place, silly girl.'

It served me right that it had been taken. He also wondered if I was telling the truth. Where would I get a sovereign? One of the girls confirmed that I had shown it to her. The teacher gave me a look of annoyance. I was holding everyone up. I was so upset that I stopped being afraid.

'My dad will be very angry if I go home without my coin,' I said, bravely. 'It's very valuable.'

'That's why you should not have brought it!' he shouted.

By now, everyone was looking troubled, but one boy suddenly stood up. His family were very well off compared to most of the children there. They frequently had foreign holidays.

'Sir, I have one of those sovereigns in my special coin wallet,' he stated. 'I've had it a long time. My grandfather gave it to me when I was ten.'

Well, we all knew he had a special coin wallet, leather with little round holes to display each coin, but I could not remember seeing a gold sovereign. However, the teacher completely accepted what he said without question and was about to dismiss the class, but fear had made me brave.

'Let me see it,' I demanded. He refused.

'It's only a gold sovereign. You couldn't know that it was yours! How could a dirty Gypsy afford a gold sovereign, anyway?'

'I would know it if I saw it!'

The teacher had had enough.

'A coin is a coin. You couldn't tell just by looking,' he sighed.

'I can.'

Frowning, he turned to the boy, who was now grinning widely.

'Well, boy, what have you to say?'

'It's my coin. A plain gold sovereign.'

'Well,' he turned back to me, 'and what have you to say?'

'It's not plain gold,' I said firmly. 'There's a small black mark on it in the shape of a nose.'

He took the wallet from the boy and examined the coin. Without a word he handed it straight to me. He said he was sorry for doubting me, while the red-faced boy was now in tears and told him he would be having a word with his parents. The next day I received a note of apology from the parents, but from the boy I had nothing.

When I returned home that afternoon, I handed the sovereign back to my father and told him everything. He took back the coin without a word, but on my fifteenth birthday he gave me another on a gold chain, and I have it still.

What a struggle it must have been for my dear mother, bringing up four children in a tiny caravan. She had very few possessions, and very little money. Thankfully, my granny and aunties shared what they could, and Mum shared what she had with all of her children. We were brought up to share with each other. We wouldn't even eat an apple in front of another child without offering to share it. But how Mum kept us dressed I will never know. She had very few clothes, but she was so tiny she looked nice in anything. She used to make my dresses by hand. Gingham was only threepence or sixpence a yard, so I was all right for clothes.

It was harder for the boys. Most of their clothes were stuff that Granny had begged from the people she sold her flowers and pegs to, so sometimes they looked a little odd, to say the least. My poor brother Nelson was always a frail boy, tall, thin and pale-looking. Granny gave Mum a parcel of clothing for him she had begged one day. Mum was pleased, until she saw what was inside: a man's evening coat with satin lapels cut away into swallow tails, striped trousers and a pair of black patent-leather shoes with buttons up the side. Mum did what she could to make them fit our Nelson by stuffing the toes of the shoes with tissue and taking up the trousers. She had tears in her eyes, but she had done her best. She knew he would look a sketch, but she had no choice and, poor boy, neither did he. When he was dressed for school the next day he looked like an over-dressed scarecrow. My little brothers were too young to realise anything was amiss, but smiled at him. I couldn't look at him. I knew what he would have to face at school. Because he was a quiet boy, he was often bullied anyway. He was about nine or ten at the time. The teacher he had was a bully as well.

On the way to school that day he was made fun of and laughed at because of those clothes, although some of the boys looked pretty bad themselves in their older brothers' cut-down jackets and trousers. My heart ached for him. He was used to being picked on, and he never answered back as he knew he wasn't strong enough to fight them. He just looked straight ahead, his face turning whiter and whiter as we went into the schoolyard.

Straight away the teacher picked on him. I was in the same class at the time, being eleven months older.

'What have we here, then?' she crowed. 'All dressed up and nowhere to go? Are you going to give us a song and dance then, boy?'

Nelson said nothing, just looked straight in front of him. However, I was getting angrier by the minute. To give the class credit, no one laughed but just sat there, glad it wasn't them, I suppose.

'Right,' said the teacher, chalking different words on the board, 'spell out and tell me these words.' She pointed at Nelson.

'What's this?' she questioned, pointing at the word 'pudding'.

'Pudden,' Nelson replied, gazing downwards. She raised her eyes ceilingward and sighed.

'No, stupid boy, "pud-*ding*"! Say it again.'

This went on for some time, Nelson getting whiter, his jaw clenched.

'Say "pud".'

'Pud,' he repeated.

'Now say "ing".'

'Ing.'

'Now say, "pudding".'

'Pudden,' said Nelson. This time, the whole class burst into raucous laughter, but I had had enough.

'Leave my brother alone!' I demanded. 'He's doing his best!'

I caught hold of his hand and sat next to him for the rest of the day. What a stoic he was. He wore those clothes for the rest of the term, and never deigned to reply to the jokes that were hurled against him. He died when he was only forty-nine, frail in body, but many a man might have envied his strength of mind.

If I seem hard on my teachers, I can only say that the ones who were nice to us were exceptional. Some did their best, and the ones who looked after the infants' class were very motherly and often kind. The trouble is, they did not understand us at all, and treated us as though we were another species.

Being a Gypsy was very different in many ways, which did make things difficult for us, but that is who we were. We must have seemed very strange to the teachers, and maybe it seems as though they were unkind all of the time, but of course they were not. They struggled to understand our ways, and often did not succeed. We in turn found it hard to understand them. Many of the poorer children were discriminated against as well as us.

I now realise that some of the little girls I went to school with were even poorer than we were, and just as strangely dressed. Clothing was passed down from parent to child, cut down and renovated. One little girl, who was thin and quiet, came to school in a pair of knee-high button boots that were fashionable in the twenties. They were a creamy colour with pointed toes, high heels and dozens of tiny buttons up the sides. They were really beautiful boots, but not at all suitable for a five-year-old. They were also much too big, and she could hardly walk in them. Eventually the teacher noticed and told her to take them off. The child struggled for ages with those buttons, and was in floods of tears by the time she had finished. She slowly pulled them off to reveal swollen, bleeding feet and no socks. The teacher must have felt some pity for her, as she kindly told her to sit near the fire. Unfortunately, everyone could see her poor feet, which upset her all the more. She sat barefoot all day, and when it was home time she could not even get the boots on, much less do all the tiny buttons up. A few of us tried to help, but the poor girl was in such distress that we had to stop. The teacher's face betrayed the fact that she wished she had left well alone. She told the girl to stay behind, and that one of the other teachers would take her home in his car. We could tell the girl did not want this to happen.

'Please, just let me walk home barefoot!' she begged.

'You can't walk home barefoot in this weather, girl! Someone will take you home.' The teacher was firm.

After that, she was away from school for some weeks, and never wore the boots again when she returned.

Poppy Day was a time we found difficult. It was a penny for the smallest poppy and a shilling for the largest. So the wealthiest children wore large ones on their jumpers, and the poorest the penny ones. These poppies then became a statement of wealth in the school. I never had a poppy at all, so what did this say about me? I never bothered about not having a poppy. I could always make a flower if I wanted to. Even so, because of being discriminated against by some, the kindness of others stands out and is long remembered.

Maybe we did go without many things, but people in general were the poorer back then, especially during the war and just after. Lots of people in our village were poor; even the shopkeepers had trouble keeping afloat. Many times I watched my more affluent schoolfriends making their purchases in the village shop for just a penny or two, but as far as I was concerned, it may as well have been pounds.

One day, the corner shop had some pencil rubbers in stock at tuppence each. This was a thrill to me. What child doesn't like to rub out mistakes, or rub out just for the joy of it? And everyone had one, except me. I had no money at all. Suddenly, as I gazed longingly at the display, a pretty woman smiled at me and said, 'Would you like a rubber?'

'Oh, yes please!'

She made her purchase and placed it in my grubby hands. I felt so unbelievably happy over this small, kind gesture, I have never forgotten it. Not all the *gadjes* I met were unkind. On another occasion I got on a crowded bus. It was a hot, sticky day and I felt I looked a sight in my shabby dress and sandals. I stood, as there were no seats.

Unexpectedly, a young, heavily made-up woman in a lovely white dress made her boyfriend shove up and patted the space beside her for me to sit down. I did so, but I was afraid I would mess up her clean white dress. She chatted away to me so kindly I forgot my shyness. As I got up to alight from the bus, she squeezed my hand in hers and said goodbye. I looked into my palm and saw that she had given me a half-crown – a fortune to me!

As soon as I got home, I breathlessly told my mother what had happened and tried to give her the money, but she would not take it.

'Just for once,' she said, 'spend it on yourself. That's what she would have wanted you to do.'

That weekend I took my brothers to the pictures, so we all enjoyed that kind lady's bounty. These kindnesses were so few, yet so profound to me I have never forgotten them.

Mr Light was the village blacksmith. He was strong

and tall, as you would expect him to be. His house was painted white with large black-painted cartwheels on the walls, and his garden was full of flowers and apple trees. All day long he toiled at his forge, his face browned and full of laughter lines, but he was never too busy to talk to a child. We spent hours, when we should have been running errands, watching him shoe the horses. The smell of burning hair and hoof pervaded the village, mingling with all the other village smells.

Many a morning we would be running up the street, late for school, and there he would be, his face raised skyward, listening to the children singing their morning hymns in our school across the road. If Granfer looked like Jesus, then Mr Light looked like John the Baptist to me, or at least like the picture I had seen on the school wall depicting him. He once told me that his favourite hymn was 'All things bright and beautiful', so when it was my turn to choose a hymn, I always chose this one, knowing Mr Light would be listening.

He always put his spare apples and plums along his garden wall for the children to help themselves, and many a hungry child was glad of this bounty as there were many who were not privileged enough to have breakfast. He had no prejudice, and he shoed all the Gypsy horses, often bringing one back personally, so he could have a natter with Granfer. Mr Light seemed indestructible to us, and we thought he would be there for ever, but one day the forge was closed and we never saw him again. I expect he died, but we were never told as children. We were supposed to be seen and not heard in those days. But we all missed him, and often spoke of him with great affection. The forge was never opened again, but I can see him still, leaning over the wall, eyes raised heavenward, listening to his favourite hymn.

From the time I was five or six, I would run errands for my mother. She always had plenty to do. She who had so little of this world's goods made up for it by her love of flowers and plants. Even Granny, who could grow most things, had to admit that Mum had green fingers, so if she had time to spare she would be in her garden, which was very long and narrow. In which, to her joy and delight, grew a peach tree that once bore six lovely peaches that were shared between us. They tasted very good, and quite a different taste to the ones we have today; much better, we all said.

Often I collected cuttings from the different places I happened to be in. I would nip a cutting from the school garden and did not, then or now, believe it to be stealing. After all, I reasoned, all plants belong to God, and I know he wouldn't mind me having a sprig or two.

Many times complete strangers, on seeing me admiring their plants, gave me a sprig of something. Gardeners are a species on their own, and don't mind sharing their plants even with a little Gypsy kid. Most of them seemed to find me amusing, perhaps quaint, but when I asked for 'a bit of that plant for my mum', they were more than pleased to share with me.

Yes, I remember many kind acts from complete strangers. One in particular I remember very clearly. If it happened to a young child today, the police would be called to get on the case. Yet it was so charming and innocent.

Mum had sent me on an errand to the small shop and post office in the village, about a mile and a half away from our camp. It was a boiling-hot summer day, the buses were full to bursting (as always in those days) and I was very hot and terribly thirsty. I bought Mum's bit of shopping and the old man who ran the shop, Mr Hobb, gave me a few sweets, as he always did. He was a lovely man, but I just couldn't bring myself to ask for a drink as well, and I certainly couldn't waste Mum's money on pop. I'll just have to wait until I get home, I thought. I hoped Mum had boiled up some water so I could have a drink at once. If she hadn't, then without telling her I would drink it anyway, as by now I was so thirsty I could almost *see* the drink I would be having soon.

The next bus and the next was standing-room only. I felt dizzy, but what could I do? Suddenly a red sports car pulled up in front of the post office. A young man got out of the car, tall, slim and very handsome, with a moustache. I noticed him at once, because Clark Gable was my cousins' pin-up and I thought him much nicer-looking than Clark Gable. He went into the shop and I looked up the road for my bus.

All at once I saw him coming across the road towards me with a large tumbler of lemonade. He smiled at me, and handed me the glass. Without any thought of saying no, I grasped the glass in both hands and gulped the contents down. No drink, before or after, had tasted so good! I finished it, gave a loud burp and he laughed as he walked back to his car. With a little wave he drove off. He was a gentleman. He had obviously felt thirsty himself and, seeing the bus pass me by, realised how thirsty I must have been. I have never forgotten his kindness, and noted that he didn't try to offer me a lift or even chat to me. He just gave me a lovely smile when I thanked him.

When I told my mother later, she said he must have been an angel. Well, he was to me.

I believe we had the most wonderful childhood, but of course we knew that people in the village looked down on us. My dad and uncles always went to the village pub, and on the whole they were treated well enough. My mother never did like my father drinking. She begrudged him his daily pint. She felt the money was better spent on the family for food and clothes, but she rarely complained. It was the only recreation the working men had; that and a game of darts. Dad enjoyed a game very much, and was in the local darts team. Once or twice a year he brought home a small trophy which his team had won, but most pubs had a sign outside which said 'No Gypsies', among others.

I have never felt ashamed that I am a Gypsy, nor will I ever allow anyone make me feel ashamed. I came from a wonderful mix of people, many who could walk with princes, some born with wonderful talents and abilities and some with the kindest hearts that you could ever meet. These above all I remember with love, and they made each day exciting, always. There was always something new and fresh to brighten our days, but sometimes these things made life a little difficult.

We accepted that we would be looked down upon by those who thought they were better than us. Granfer had almost given us a superiority complex; at least, among our schoolmates, as he continually told us we were as good as they were, if not better. We needed this, as we were constantly put down. He admired everything we did; our every small achievement. He told the girls they were beautiful and the boys that they were handsome. Our parents always did their best to send us to school clean and tidy, and we were certainly no worse than the other children.

It was a terrible shock to be told to stay after school one day by one of the female teachers. I was worried, and asked why.

'Just do as you are told,' she said firmly.

She gave me a job filling the ink wells, a job we all detested as we always got ink over our hands and on our clothes. Then she asked me to change the water in the flower vases, and left the room. I liked doing that job, except the water stank and the stems were slimy. I was beginning to get anxious. She was ages coming back. I knew my bus had gone, and that I would have to walk home. I was not concerned that Mum would be worried, because Violet would tell her where I was. I heard footsteps approaching. The door opened and the teacher who had asked me to wait swept in, holding a bulky brown-paper parcel. Another teacher followed her into the room, both looking very pleased with themselves.

'Sit down, Rosemary. We have something here for you. We hope you will be pleased.'

I waited, wondering what this was all about. I knew from experience that most teachers rarely did anything kind for us Gypsy kids. I looked up expectantly. She was so excited. Well, I thought, this must be something really good.

'You will be aware that we had a jumble sale recently, Rosemary.'

'Yes, Miss,' I nodded. I had been to the jumble sale, and bought a story book for a few pennies, but most of all I remembered the ghastly smell. Looking extremely pleased, they both opened the parcel.

'We kept some of the clothes that still had some wear in, for you, Rosemary,' she continued, holding up three of the most appalling dresses I have ever seen. They had obviously been cut down from elderly ladies' dresses. One was a dull murky shade of blue, and the other two were a brownish colour. The texture of the cloth was rough and hairy, in fact little white hairs appeared to stick out of the material. To make matters worse, there were a few pairs of silky pink and blue bloomers, the crotches of which were stained and faded, and had obviously belonged to a very fat lady. They looked at me smiling happily, and I looked back at them in horror. I felt sick. The dresses had clearly not been sold at the jumble sale as they were so vile, so why would the teachers think that I would want them? I thrust out my arms.

'No. No, I don't want they horrible frocks or they knickers. No.'

They stared at me, shock written all over their faces. Too young to be diplomatic, I continued.

'They stinks! I won't never wear *they* dirty things!'

They looked down their noses at me in unison.

'Well! I'm very surprised at you, Rosemary! You are extremely ungrateful. After all, beggars can't be choosers!'

Tears filled my eyes, but I would not let them see how I felt. I ran out of the classroom and all the way home. When I got back to the camp, my mother asked why I was kept in. I told her, thinking I would be in trouble for what I had said to the teacher, but Mum laughed until she cried.

'I'm proud of you,' she said, 'we've got enough rubbish of our own; we don't need theirs!'

The next day, I went to school in nervous anticipation of what they might say or do. Neither teacher said anything, and the parcel was still on the table behind them. I tried not to look, but I felt sick with apprehension as I wondered if they would try and force me to take the clothes home, but I felt more shocked and sick by what happened next.

The class was told to sit down, as the vicar was coming in to give us a little talk. I was not worried. I knew and liked him, as he had always been pleasant to all the children. He breezed in and smiled his benevolent smile.

'I am going to talk to you today about gratitude and ingratitude.'

He went on to talk at length about my behaviour in the face of the kindness that had been shown to me. Oh, he was very careful not to name me, but every so often he would stare at me piercingly. I sat there quietly, feeling very cold. In conclusion, he said a prayer that I could not bring myself to join in. As we all filed past him to return to our classrooms, he placed his hand on each child's head and blessed them. I made up my mind that he was not going to bless *me*. I sat there until I was the last to leave, and then walked around the other side of the room. As I was going out of the door, he called me back, but I took no notice and left the room. Nothing was ever said to me about this, but when I came home from school one day, my mother told me that the vicar had been to see her.

'He spoke well of your schoolwork,' she said. I did not reply.

'He came to ask me a favour.'

I looked at her, surprised. What would a vicar want of Gypsy folk?

'It's Mothering Sunday next week. He asked me if I would make a few dozen penny bunches of primroses for the schoolchildren to buy for their mothers for Mother's Day.'

She had agreed politely, not realising the work that this would entail. She spent most of Saturday looking for and picking the flowers, then sat up almost the whole night making tiny nosegays. The next morning she walked all the way to the church to deliver them. I must admit, they did look very nice, arranged on a bed of fresh moss. Mum was paid about one pound for all her hard work and a night's lost sleep, and I wondered if the vicar had given a thought about my mother and how

246

hard she had worked simply because she did not know how to say no to someone who considered himself superior to her. I never did anything he asked me to do. When he visited the school, as he did twice a month, I stayed away until the afternoon. In the past, he had often asked me to read at the morning service, his eyebrows expressing amazement at how well I could read – for a Gypsy. His expression said it all. I never did read again after that. I said I had a sore throat, or stayed at home.

Shortly after the nosegay business, my mother became very ill with pleurisy. I stayed home from school to take care of her for a few days until my Aunt Brit was able to help. I was still quite young, and the most I could do was to get her cold drinks and keep her company until my father came home. I liked being with her, but her harsh breathing scared me and I wanted an adult there. Brit walked me to school the following week to explain that my mother had been ill. She had gone to the school years before, and knew some of the older teachers. She spotted the teacher who had tried to give me the jumble-sale clothes and told her I had been away because my mother was so ill. She smiled, and said that she understood. Quick as a flash, I said my piece.

'The doctor told my mother that she should not have ruined her health just to make the vicar look good with his "tricksy" little nosegays! Let his wife and kids do it in future!' I quoted.

I knew for sure that this would reach the vicar's ears sooner or later, and I felt vindicated and very pleased with myself. Poor Brit was shocked at what I had said, but she said she understood how angry I was and she felt the same as me. After all, I had my pride.

New Beginnings and Fond Farewells

My young cousins, who were aged between fourteen and nineteen, would sit around the camp fire on a summer's evening and sing all the songs they knew, and then repeat them over and over again. The fire blazed, sending sparks into the night sky while they laughed, told stories, sometimes shed a few tears, quickly forgotten with hugs and cuddles. These young girls had nothing better than the company of each other, but when they got together it was magical. Many a summer's night I drifted off to sleep listening to their sweet voices raised in song.

They had a metal hair iron which they would heat up on Granny's range, wrap their hair around, wait for a few seconds and then unwrap to reveal glorious curls. The smell of burning hair was overpowering. We all started coughing and choking. I held my nose.

"Ee be ruining yer 'air, our Mary. Why 'ee can't plait it, like, I do not know,' Granny commented. Mary cast her a disparaging look.

'That's old-fashioned, our mam. I'd be laughed at if I did me 'air like yours!'

Granfer sat up in his chair.

'Show yer mother some respect. My Mary Ann *always* looks beautiful.'

Mary unwrapped her hair from the hot curling iron and the beautiful burned-off curl fell neatly into the palm of her hand. The iron, of course, was far too hot.

'I told 'ee, our Mary,' sighed Granny. 'If 'ee keeps that game up, 'ee'll be bald!'

The thought of Mary bald-headed sent us into a fit of laughter, but Mary looked very upset. So, no more was said. She put a piece of elastic around her head and rolled her hair into what she called a 'victory roll'. I thought it looked very nice. Far better than the curls she had been trying to force her hair into. It was Betty's turn next. She curled the top into large sausage curls and then, holding them in place with large hairpins, she produced a bottle of brilliantine and proceeded to anoint the back of her hair with it. It smelled very powerful.

'This is called "Ashes of Roses",' she said.

'Gawd!' sniggered my cousin Johnny. 'It smells more like ashes of rubbish heaps!'

Mary was not in the mood for this, and she rounded on him in a rage.

'What would you know, you silly boy! Wait till you gets a gelfriend, you won't be sayin' things like that then!'

'Well, I ain't never gonna 'ave a gel. I'se keepin' all me money fer me own self. I ain't spendin' it on some gel who only wants me fer me money!'

Mary shrugged, and proceeded to comb Betty's hair but the brilliantine had made it so greasy that nothing could be done with it. What with the smell and the grease, her hair had to be washed again, but the smell hung around for days, causing everyone who came in to ask, 'Gawd! What's that horrible smell?'

While the brilliantine was supposed to give a healthy shine (with moderate use), the same could be said for the stuff the men and boys plastered their hair with. My own father never used it, but the others, not being able to read the instructions for use, put huge dollops of it on their hair, whereupon it ruined everything it touched and made lots of washing. If the men had been doing dirty work, the oil in their hair mixed with the dirt and dust. Then, after a hard day, they would lean back on the armchairs and leave behind a filthy, oily residue. This caused many hot words between the women and their menfolk. After a while, the men decided not to use this awful hair cream, and peace reigned once more.

In common with most girls, young or old, Gypsy or *gadje*, we all liked things that smelled nice. 'Ooh,' we would say on smelling a perfumed rose or some cheap scent, 'that do be a lovely smell, real scenty!'

We would sprinkle ourselves liberally with any concoction that fitted this description. Unfortunately, our elders did not appreciate these heady odours as much as we did.

I was given a bottle of jasmine scent as a gift. Even I thought it was a bit strong, but I thought that, being out in the fresh air, it would die down a bit. Waiting for the school bus the next morning, I very kindly shared it among six of us little girls.

'Ooh, Rosie, yer do smell lovely an' scenty!' remarked Violet.

To tell the truth, I felt a bit sick, the scent was so heavy. Half an hour later, we were on our way home. The teachers did not think we smelled scenty, and neither did the bus driver.

The greatest treat of the year for my older cousins and young aunts was a trip to Bridgwater Fair. They saved every penny they could so that each could buy a special outfit. Dressing up for the fair was not as strange as it sounds. It was not the fair itself that they wanted to visit, but it was the social occasion that was so important. They met up with all the other young men and women from the travelling folk at this fair, so they wanted to look their very best. These days, people would dress in jeans and wellies to go to the fair, but the Gypsy girls would dress up in the hope of attracting a boyfriend or future husband. We little ones admired them as they came out of their wagons in their finery, and told them how beautiful they looked, which they certainly did.

The men and boys always drove the young girls to the fair in their lorries, and kept a strict eye on them when they got there. The girls were taken care of as if they were princesses, which they were to their families. They were allowed a weak drink or two, but that was all. Any other drinks were lemonade or squash. They were allowed to dance with the young lads within the fair's travelling community, but it was very rare for any of these short acquaintances to lead to marriage. At these fairs, old feuds surfaced among the young, leading to fist fights. Many a young man went off with a thick lip or a black eye, and yet shortly after they would be buying each other drinks and joking together. This fair was held annually, and was eagerly looked forward to and talked about for weeks before and after. There were many booths showing things that would never be seen now, such as The Bearded Lady, The Two-Headed Man, Real Dwarves and The Fat Lady. The booth that interested the men in my family the most was the boxing ring. I learned from one of my cousins that my father used to fight in these booths, and often won. He said Dad was a very good bare-knuckle boxer, and the only reason he went to the fair was to 'enjoy a few rounds in the ring'. The prize was five pounds for managing to stay on your feet for five rounds. Apparently Dad rarely lost, and would go home with a pocketful of money and a split lip. My cousin made me smile when he told me that Dad went ten rounds without any training, and then decided to have a go on his mate's motorbike. Unfortunately, at the same time the local priest was coming in through the gates escorting several young nuns, and Dad's attention was diverted momentarily by this unusual sight. He lost control of the machine, which he had never driven in his life, and mowed down the priest, narrowly avoiding the nuns. The priest only had a few bumps and bruises.

'Anyone less like a man of God I've yet to meet,' said Dad. ''Is language was colourful, to say the least!'

The priest raised his fists and threatened to beat Dad up.

'Go home and behave yourself,' said an onlooker.

'He's just gone ten rounds with nine bare-knuckle box-
ers!'

With a last angry shout, the priest ushered the weeping nuns out of the fairground. Dad called the youngest
nun back and gave her one of the five-pound notes he
had won.

''Ere, 'ave this,' he said. 'Spend it on treats fer the
littl'uns. It was my fault yer day was spoiled.'

For most people, this incident would have ruined
their day, but not Dad. No one was really hurt, and he
had a good story to tell down the pub for weeks to come
and a bit of extra money to take home to my mother.
She hated him bare-knuckle boxing, and told him he
would be killed one day. Dad was a stranger to worry,
though. He left all that to others, considering it to be a
waste of time. He truly believed that laughter was the
best medicine, and always had a joke or a funny story to
tell. When he reached the punch line, his laughter
would bounce off the walls and float off into the distance. My mother, however, would do the worrying for
everyone.

'Don't you *ever* worry, Eddy?' she asked, after tending
to yet another cut eyebrow after a night at the fair. He
sat in profound thought, forehead creased, trilby well
back on his head, and uttered his own proverbial saying.

'Why worry? 'Ee'll die if 'ee worries and 'ee'll die if 'ee
don't!'

In fact, I have no idea how my cousins or aunts met their
partners. No one had been happier than Granny when
Nelson finally came home from the war for good.

Shortly after he was demobbed, he met a pretty woman named Rene. She was not Romany but she was Scottish, which we found fascinating. Granny was not happy at all when he announced that he wanted to marry her. Granny did not want him to marry anyone, preferring him to remain single, but he had his way, and bought a trailer (caravan) and lived in the paddock across the road. Later on he built a wooden bungalow, and they turned it into a comfortable home where my cousins and I would spend many fun-filled hours babysitting their many beautiful children. Rene was not much older than us, and we learned about *gadje* ways from her, and she in turn learned to live as a Romany. They lived very happily, so Granny had to accept it in the end, but she would have preferred all her children to have married 'in the same blood', as she thought it made life easier.

Violet and I enjoyed babysitting for Uncle Nelson and Rene. Brenda was their first child. She was beautiful and it was a pleasure to look after her, but one night we had a bad scare. As Rene and Uncle Nelson's place was across the road from us in the paddock, it was not far to go and we were within earshot of family. Violet and I were curled up on the sofa. It was a very quiet night; you could almost hear a pin drop. Suddenly the light dimmed in the room. It often did this, so at first we took no notice. Then, we seemed to hear all sorts of noises; creaking and little bangs.

'Look, Rosie!' Violet whispered.

'What?'

My heart was beating like a drum as she pointed to

the partly open door of Rene and Uncle Nelson's bedroom. I squinted in the gloom to see.

'Look! Look!' she quavered. 'There's a Chinaman lying on the bed and . . . 'e's lookin' at us!'

By now, I was shaking like a leaf. You might say, what a silly thing to think. Why on earth should a Chinaman be lying on the bed looking at us? It just shows how strong is the power of suggestion and an overactive, childish imagination. The more I looked, the more I could see the Chinaman. How long we sat there in frozen silence I do not know, but it was just as well the baby did not wake up as I knew very well that we could not have gone in to her. When we heard the key turn in the lock, we both burst into tears of relief.

'What? What's happened?' asked Rene fearfully. 'Is the baby all right? Why is it dark in here?'

With shaking hands, we both pointed silently to the bedroom door. Puzzled, Uncle Nelson pushed it open and switched the light on. Immediately, feeling very silly, we both realised that the Chinaman was Rene's new embroidered yellow silk bedspread! The way it was creased on the bed made it look like a Chinaman, even down to his eyes and little round hat with a tassel on top. Now laughing with relief, we explained why we were so scared, but they were both perplexed. They just could not see what we had thought we had seen, but it had seemed real enough to us.

We still babysat for the children. Both with rosy cheeks and black curls, they were the apple of their parents' eyes. Rene was very young at heart. She laughed at our way of speaking, and we laughed at hers, but it was all good-natured. We found her accent end-lessly amusing, and tried to copy it as we waited for her to get ready to go out with Uncle Nelson at the week-end. She was slim, and often mourned the loss of her bosom due to having two children. However, nothing daunted, she filled her bra with socks or cotton wool and stuck a tea leaf to her cheek as a make-believe beauty spot. She looked very pretty, we thought.

When she came home she laughed as she recounted how her beauty spot had fallen off while she had been talking to someone. On another occasion, while dan-cing, the socks fell out of her bra. She roared with laughter, and soon had us laughing as well. She was shocked on passing a pub with a sign saying No Gypsies Allowed, so they came straight home and dressed in the best clothes they had. Rene had told Uncle Nelson firmly: 'If you are good enough t' fight for this country, then you're good enough to go into this country's pubs!'

Uncle Nelson was a very handsome man and with his black curls, dark eyes and beautiful teeth he looked wonderful. So did Rene. They walked into that pub as if they owned it. Not a word was said to them either then or any time after that.

Uncle Nelson had a Chrysler car which only carried two or three people comfortably, but that did not stop them loading the car so that it sank inches lower than it was supposed to. It was a very old car, and Uncle Nelson knew it was too small for the family when he bought it, but it had a boot with a door that pulled down from the top, so he would wedge the adults in the car and then five or six little children in the boot with our heads sticking out of the top. We children loved it, but it could not have been legal, even then. We were never stopped by the police, but there was hardly any traffic in those days.

Rene and Nelson had seven children eventually, although one girl died as a baby, but she was still part of the family to them. They had been born into a different way of life, but no one could have been happier than they. Rene often baked cakes while chatting to Violet and me, as though we were all the same age. She was great fun, and I often think of those happy times and they make me smile.

When my Aunty Brit and Uncle Tom got married, they had nowhere to live so they bought an old scrap coach and transformed it into a warm and comfortable home. All of their children were born in this coach, and they were very happy there. It was almost like a little bungalow. Many years later, Uncle Tom was knocked off his motorbike and nearly lost his life. He bought a little farmhouse with his compensation and they lived there, not far from the camp, for the rest of their lives, and now one of his daughters lives there still with her family.

My Aunty Brit has passed away now, but I will always remember her. I have a lovely old photograph of her aged about fifteen, sitting on Aunt Prissy's caravan steps. Granfer is sitting just below her with lots of small children at his feet and a baby on his lap, looking so happy and smiling, the happiness emanates from the photograph.

She married her lovely Tom when she was about

twenty-five; a true love match. He was an Irishman who came to England to mend the roads. He was softly spoken, with amazing blue eyes and black curly hair. Aunty Brit still had time for us, and would join in our games.

One day something happened that would haunt me for years. I asked her to play a game that involved a paper triangle, the corners folded to conceal the answers. First, I happily asked her for her favourite colour. After much thought she said, 'Blue.' Then a number. 'Three.' After some fiddling with the folded paper, I laughed triumphantly.

'You are going to have three blue babies!'

She joined in my laughter as, after all, it was only a joke.

Time passed, and then one day she told us she would soon be having a baby! We were so happy. What a blessed baby to have Brit for its mother.

One morning as we awoke, Mum told us that Brit had had her baby – a beautiful baby girl! Brit and Tom were going to name her Kathleen (my mother's name, although everyone called her Mary).

We couldn't wait to see the new baby, and as soon as we came home from school, Mum made us wash our hands and faces. Clutching a shiny two-shilling piece for the baby 'to bring her luck', we trotted off to see the new arrival.

Mum had told us she was beautiful, and so she was. We gazed at her in awe. She had pale skin, black curls and blue eyes and Aunty Brit looked so beautiful as she gazed at her new baby daughter, her eyes full of love.

Tom held Brit's hand as he watched his firstborn. Lucky, lucky baby to have such wonderful parents.

The very next day, we jumped off the school bus happy and excited at the thought of seeing baby Kathleen. When we got to the gate, Mum was waiting for us. She put her finger to her lips.

'Be quiet,' she said softly. 'Aunty Brit's baby girl has died.'

I was numb with shock at this dreadful news, but worse was to come.

'How did the baby die?' I asked incredulously.

'She was a blue baby.'

I felt sick. My ears started to sing. Everything whirled around me. What had I done? I had killed Brit's baby girl! I had told her she would have a blue baby, so it was my fault that baby Kathleen had died. I was devastated, but I told no one. How could I ever confess to the terrible thing that I had done?

Days and months passed, and I still grieved. Aunty Brit was soon up and about and looked a little like her old self, although a sad look crossed her face whenever she saw a newborn baby. Three years passed until Aunty Brit had her second child, and I was three years older, but I still firmly believed that it was my fault that her firstborn had died.

Mum said, 'Go and see Aunty Brit's baby.'

I made every excuse I could think of not to go. Finally I ran out of them and I went, but I was terrified to look at the baby. When I did, I saw a perfect little child with pink and white skin, black curly hair and long, long eyelashes. She didn't look like a blue baby, but I still fretted. Finally, my mother, who had noticed my misery, had had enough.

'What on earth is wrong with you?' she demanded. 'Every time I look at you, you look the picture of misery. What is it? Tell me!'

It all came flooding out. It was my fault baby Kathleen had died. If only I hadn't played that stupid, stupid game. I had told Aunty Brit that she would have a blue baby – and she had! Now I was terrified that her second baby would suffer the same fate as well. In fact, I had told her she would have *three* blue babies! One had already died, and now I was worried to death that this baby would die as well, and it would be all my fault. I burst into tears. When would this misery stop?

Mum looked really shocked and upset. I could hardly look at her for shame.

'Have you felt like this all this time?'

'Yes,' I whimpered.

'My dear child, it's not your fault the baby died. She was born very ill, with holes in her heart, and her blood couldn't circulate around her tiny little body. That's why she looked blue, not because of anything you said.'

Mum gave me a hug, and I burst into tears of relief. I almost couldn't believe it wasn't my fault after all. Aunty Brit's new baby would not die, but grow healthy and strong. It was true. I could stop blaming myself and get on with my life. It may seem strange that I should believe that I was responsible for the baby's death, but things were very different back then. In many ways, we were backward and kept in the dark about childbirth and associated problems. Superstition was a big part of our lives too.

Aunty Brit went on to have four healthy children after the death of Kathleen, three girls and then a boy, a little blessing who arrived when she was aged forty-five. I have never forgotten that first lovely child, though, here for just a short time but who had a profound effect on us all.

Granny's strange *vardoe* came to a very sad end one autumn evening. I looked out of our caravan window when a bright orange light caught my eye. It was flickering on the roof of the caravan. I watched for several minutes, wondering what it was. Then Mum followed my gaze.

'Fire!' she screamed. 'Fire! Fire!'

By then the fire had got a firm hold, and despite many buckets of water, nothing was saved. In the morning only a pile of ash and twisted metal remained where the strange caravan once stood.

Granny, however, was broken-hearted at the loss of her *vardoe*. Granfer did his best to console her, but nothing worked. She mourned the destruction of her lovely things. Even her crystal ball had been destroyed. Granfer was at a loss for what to do. Granny had eaten nothing for days. So Granfer, who cooked his breakfast over the camp fire every morning, decided to cook her some eggs fresh from the hens, and gave up his own bacon ration. It looked very nice and smelled wonderful. When he had finished, he called her.

'Mary Ann! Mary Ann! I've got something for 'ee.'

Seeing her come, he sprinkled the meal with salt and pepper and what he thought was brown sauce. It wasn't. Granfer couldn't read, and so had liberally sprinkled Camp Coffee over the new-laid eggs and fresh bacon. Granny instantly recognised the bottle, and so did we. We wondered what would happen next.

'There, Mary Ann,' said Granfer, looking at her with much love and compassion. 'There, there, eat up your grub and 'ee'll feel better.'

Granny, that little firebrand of a woman, meekly sat down and ate every mouthful while Granfer looked on, full of joy because his Mary Ann would soon be herself.

As far as I know, nothing was ever said to Granfer. We all loved him too much to hurt his feelings. Mary Ann, who soon regained her energy, looked at him with a twinkle in her little black eyes, and when he asked her if she had enjoyed her meal, she told him it was the best meal she had ever tasted; in fact, it would be a long time before she forgot it. So Granfer was happy and Granny was her old self again.

The day that Granfer died started just like any other. Granfer had got up early and lit the camp fire, putting the big black kettle over it to boil. No one had noticed he was not there after that, so Granny made the tea. I had woken early and was out by the fire, so Granny handed me his mug.

'Granfer's layin' down fer a bit. Let 'im 'ave 'is rest.'

I took the mug from her, and my aunt Mary followed me in and pushed the door open for me to Granfer's room. Granfer was lying on his bed, and he turned his head towards me as I placed the tea carefully on the cupboard beside him.

'Thank 'ee, my pretty,' he said.

As I turned to leave the room, I heard Mary gasp, and pushing me gently out of the room, she called out to Granny.

'Mam! Mam, come quick! Dad's gone!'

Granny appeared in the doorway of the hut, and hurried into Granfer's room. Then, Granny came back out.

'He's gone,' she whispered. 'My Edwin's gone.'

We were all shocked and quiet. It was hard to understand, especially for me, how one minute he was there and the next minute he was not. We just sat waiting for the doctor to arrive. When he came, he did not stay long in Granfer's room but held Granny's hand for a while. He was a delightful man.

'We will all miss him, Mrs Penfold.'

'Thank 'ee. I knows 'ee 'as always done yer best.'

'Yes, and I will certainly miss the cough sweets!'

So, dear Granfer died shortly after drinking his morning tea laced with a generous tot of whisky. It poured with rain all that day, and I felt this was how it should be. I wanted the rain to last for ever. Why should we who loved him so much be the only ones who cried? What an empty space! What would we do without him telling us his tales, some very tall ones among them? Most were true, though, and all very funny.

The animals looked for him, the cats were crying and the dogs whining, but most of all his horses missed him. They called and whinnied all that wet rainy day.

Granny just sat. No going out with her basket today, but she packed it anyway, then she unpacked it and packed it yet again. She picked up Granfer's snuff box.

'I bought this fer my Edwin at Bampton Fair, from an old traveller who said 'e remembered me from when I was a young gal. I didn't believe 'im but I bought the box because my Edwin liked 'is snuff.'

Looking at her tearful eyes was heartbreaking.

''E always called me "Mary Ann". 'E liked my name.'

She stood up, and, picking up his little silver comb and curling his kiss curl around her finger, she tucked the comb into his fingers for the last time and slowly turned away.

The doctor was so right about Granfer being missed. I do not think I have ever stopped missing him. He left a big space when he died, and no one has ever filled it. He died as gently and as peacefully as he had lived.

Granny commented sadly that now there was no one left to call her Mary Ann. I stood by Granny as she looked upon him in his coffin. He looked so young. She moved the kiss curl into the centre of his forehead and kissed his cheek.

''E was the only man I ever kissed,' she whispered. ''E was a good man, my Edwin. Yes, 'e was.'

The day of Granfer's funeral came all too soon. The wreaths and bouquets covered every available surface. Some had to be laid on the wash-house floor.

Many Gypsy families who knew us came to stay a few days; others came just for the day. Although I was very young, I well remember the overwhelmingly heavy scent of the flowers and the many shapes of the wreaths.

Granny had ordered a big car for Granfer's coffin. As I saw the shiny black hearse swing slowly into the yard, I thought of the very few times Granfer had ever been in a car. He really liked them, though, and I could almost hear him gently laugh at his Mary Ann.

'Mary Ann, still wasting your money on me, then?' he would have said. As usual, she would have smiled and said nothing.

The funeral cortège stretched from our camp to the long drive of the church, maybe a mile and a half. There were Gypsy wagons, horses, carts and some cars all holding up the traffic as three young policemen stood on the pavement's edge, waving the cortège through so as to allow Granfer's last 'voyage' to continue unimpeded.

Suddenly, as Granfer's coffin passed by, the young policemen snapped to attention, removed their helmets and bowed their heads. I was deeply touched by this, but I could almost hear Granfer's laugh and his voice say, 'Looks like they've forgiven me, then, for all the poachin' they tried to nab me fer!'

The day passed by at last, and everyone had something nice to say about Granfer. There was laughter as well as tears, his life was toasted with large tots of whisky and everyone got tipsy. Some even sang a song or two, and that is exactly what he would have liked, that and to always remember him with love. That I have always done.

Butterflies

As we grew older, at the ages of twelve or thirteen Betsy and Violet would go to Bridgwater Fair with their parents. There was such excitement.

'Come with us, Rosie!' they urged.

'No, I'm picking blackberries.'

'Oh, don't be a spoilsport. Won't yer mam let yer go, then?'

If I had asked my mother she would probably have let me go, as long as there was an adult with us. I was older now, and my love of the funfair had diminished a little. I saw the cheap trinkets they brought back that were thrown away in a short time, and I noticed their ruined clothes. It always seemed to be raining when the fair was on, and it was held in a muddy field. I was becoming more self-aware, and decided that I would have been so worried about spoiling the few best clothes and shoes I had that I would have been rendered incapable of enjoying myself. At that time I was totally uninterested in the idea of dressing up to attract boys. We were much too young; little more than children. The only boys we saw day to day were our cousins and the boys at school. We regarded them as just somebody's brother, and romance was the domain of mature actors and actresses on the silver screen, too far removed from reality for us.

But there was no holding back time. The years were speeding by far too quickly. I was fifteen years old when I agreed to have my ears pierced. All my girl cousins and aunts had had earrings since the age of nine or ten, but I had always put off the decision. In the end, Dad decided for me, on my fifteenth birthday. He handed me a little box. When I opened it, nestled inside was a pair of gold earrings and a sovereign on a gold chain. Dad must have had a good week. At first I refused to have my ears pierced.

'I think I'll wait a bit,' I said. As for the sovereign, it just brought back bad memories. I was also afraid that my ears would become infected.

'Just put your earrings in straight away and turn them from the bottom. That way you won't touch your ears,' Mum advised.

Dad said that his sister Nellie would pierce my ears for me with a darning needle, as she had done for everyone else. So I was brought like a lamb to the slaughter while she pinched my ears to 'deaden the pain', so she said. She then thrust the needle through my ear. Blood spurted everywhere. I was wearing a white blouse, and this just made it look worse. I ran screaming to my mother who calmly said, 'Well, you'll have to have the other one done now!'

So back I went to repeat the performance. To this day I still wear the earrings, and have never taken them out except once, when they needed repairs which cost two pounds; exactly the amount they had cost twenty-five years earlier.

There were only four classes in the school. We were moved up as we grew older. No one was made to stay in the same class if they were old enough to move up, even though many had learned next to nothing. We seemed to learn much the same in each class. Perhaps the sums were more difficult, and we learned the most important historic dates. It was all very basic.

As I grew older, my school life became easier because I loved to write stories and compositions. I also loved memorising and reciting poetry. Because of this I often came near or top of the class, and some of my work was read out to other classes. Although I befriended a few of the *gadje* girls I could trust, I did not want them to become part of my home life and I had no curiosity about theirs. I considered school life to be a totally separate life to home, one that was inflicted upon me without any choice on my part and one which I had to get through as bearably as possible.

There were one or two exceptions, however. I was invited and went to a birthday party given by a lovely girl called Jean. She was always ready to share anything we needed in class, although she was not much better off than any of us, but in her quiet way she made us feel welcome.

I had occasionally seen a *gadje* girl across the road from the bus stop where we waited to go home. She was always dressed in a smart red blazer, as she attended a private school. I thought she looked very posh. I was extremely surprised to see her some time later sitting in the seat next to mine as I came back into class one day. She looked up and smiled at me.

'Hello, I'm Dawn. You all looked so happy and full of fun,' she explained, as she noted my expression. 'I begged my mum to let me go to your school. So, here I am!' As I slid into my seat I knew immediately we were going to be friends.

Shortly after, she invited me home for tea. In the short time I had known her she had not once made me feel uncomfortable or asked me questions about my home life, as most of the other *gadje* girls did. I found her honesty and natural manner appealing, and I opened up to her almost without realising it. I never would have with the other girls, whose motives I was suspicious of. Her family were lovely to me and made me feel at home. As I sat in her kitchen with its modest furnishings and the scent of orange blossom wafting in from the garden, I realised I had made suppositions about her before I had met her that were totally inaccurate: something others had often done to me.

During those lovely summer days when I was fourteen and fifteen, Dawn, Violet, Betsy and I spent hours walking in the woods and fields, chatting and giggling. Dawn was the only girl I could trust enough to invite home. She met all my family, and they welcomed her in the same way as her family had welcomed me. She never spoke about the way we lived, even though I knew that she was asked by some of the other schoolchildren. This infuriated some of them, as she only made our lives seem more intriguing and exciting when she refused to answer their questions.

Some time after Dawn arrived at the school we had a new headmaster, Mr Wisdom. He was very tall and thin with tightly curled hair. I had actually sat next to him on the bus going home from Dawn's house without realising it. She had picked me a huge bunch of orange blossoms from her garden to take home to my mother, and when I got on the bus he moved up to give me room.

'What a wonderful perfume!' he exclaimed, inhaling deeply.

'My friend gave them to me,' I smiled through the flowers.

'Does she live far?'

'Only in the village. I live further up the road.'

'I'm new to this area. It's very peaceful.'

'I love it here. I wouldn't want to live anywhere else.'

He chatted to me until I got off at my stop.

'See you Monday!' he called after me.

I did not know what he meant, and dismissed it from my mind until school on Monday when he was introduced as our new headmaster. I was so pleased, as he seemed much nicer than the last one, whom I had regarded with a sense of dread.

He *was* a very nice man. He treated me, my brothers and my cousins the same as everyone else, not fish of one and fowl of another. He sometimes deviated from what he was teaching to tell us of his exploits in the army. He knew how to laugh at himself, and kept us in fits of laughter.

'I met my wife when I was in the army,' he said. 'I'm

six foot four and my wife is four foot six. She didn't see my face for the first six months – she only came up to my knees! By then it was too late. We were in love!'

He came to our camp a few times. He just dropped in. I think we fascinated him. He really tried with all of us.

'I want you all to be the best you can be!' was his adage.

The material he had to work with was very poor, but he did his best. As far as possible, I actually enjoyed these last few years at school. Mr Wisdom allowed us to have parties, arranged coach trips and school dances. He also allowed us to have the schoolroom windows open on warm summer days, something our old headmaster never let us do, no matter how stifling hot it was. Sometimes he said we could have a whole afternoon of singing. I loved this, as we all did. My favourite song was 'Barbara Allen', and many of us had tears in our eyes when 'Cru-ell Barbara Allen' lay on her deathbed repenting with her last breath.

So our final days of school slowly drew to an end. Just as the days of going out hawking with heavy baskets were coming to an end, we would all do different things with our lives. My father would never have let me go out hawking at people's doors.

'You bide yer with yer mammy an' 'elp 'er,' he would say, almost as though I was a cosseted lady. Yes, the world was changing, and our lives would change with it.

I knew that I would have to earn my living, and I also wanted to help Mum a little bit, but never having had much money, I wasn't that concerned. I think my cousins felt the same. We would make our way in life somehow, and as it turned out, we all did.

When I left school, very few of us had any idea of what to do next. We had no grades or exam results of any sort. Mr Wisdom told us that he would speak for us if an employer needed it. None of my family, close or extended, had ever worked for an employer apart from a day or a week here or there, haymaking or harvesting. Dawn said it might be fun working in Woolworth's in town. We all loved that shop. We went together for a brief interview and to our surprise, we were told to start the following week. Dawn only stayed a short time, and left for a different part of the country. I only saw her once or twice after that, but I had made several new young friends. I found it easy to mix with the *gadje* girls. They were all very nice and showed me what to do and what not to do. They accepted me completely, and I suffered no prejudice at all. We sometimes went to the pictures and, later, to dances. Dad was not very happy about this at all, and worried that I was having too much freedom.

Of course, I wondered where my life was going. I knew that I would probably have to live in the *gadje* world. I was not unduly worried about this, but I always thought, and still do, that Gypsies are more fun to be with than *gadjes*. They have a wonderful sense of humour. As soon as I go to a family get-together, I am almost another person. My daughter notices this, particularly with our way of speaking. I explained it this way: when in Rome, do as the Romans. She knew what I meant.

In spite of this, I met and married my husband John when I was eighteen. Since getting married, I have lived mostly in the *gadje* world, but a great deal in the Romany one, if only in my mind. John loves the Romany way of life, and for many years we spent every weekend visiting my old home. Mum and Dad were very fond of John, and adored our four lovely children, Sarah, Virginia, and Daniel and Claire, the twins. Our second child, a son, lived for just one day. That was a very bad time for all of us. He had been born with a congenital heart disease. It took a long time to recover from the shock of it. Now our family is complete, and yet still growing. We have been blessed to have played a large part in our children's and grandchildren's lives, and most weekends will find our home bursting at the seams with family. My daughter Sarah came shopping with me one day, and as we put away the huge amount of food, she asked if I had any ambitions.

'Yes,' I replied, 'to walk around Tesco with just a basket!'

With all the visitors and family still coming, I do not think I will ever achieve this. So my house is full of jokes and laughter, and John plays his part. He builds beautiful working scale-model locomotives, and he keeps his little grandsons and the big boys entertained for hours. He makes every piece himself from scrap metal, and they are very beautiful.

Every child in turn, Sarah in particular, has listened wide-eyed to the story of two little Gypsy girls who peeped over a gate one day and beheld the wondrous sight of a field full of butterflies.

The day I left school, though, was the end of my childhood. I was just a very young fifteen-year-old, still in socks and pigtails, as were my cousins and friends. We stood at our very last assembly and sang 'Lord dismiss us with thy blessing', with the full awareness that our childhood was over and could never be reclaimed. I glanced at Violet and Dawn, and their eyes met mine. Tears tumbled down our cheeks, splashing in droplets on our school jumpers. Never did I think that I would feel so sad, or know such a sense of loss. I went home to tea with Dawn and Violet went to the pictures.

Going home after tea with Dawn, I realised that my life would now change. Would it be better out in the *gadje* world? Only time would tell. My thoughts floated back to when we were just little children. We were all grateful to have both our parents and each other. Best of all, we had Granny and Granfer. We always knew that Granfer belonged to all of us little children. We also knew that he was first of all Granny's husband, and that as a grown-up person, she was first in his affections, but we accepted this. Granny would always be busy working and making sure that things were as they should be. Granfer, however, still had time to let us help feed the chickens.

'Mind out, my pretty,' he would say. 'Don't 'ee chuck it on they poor fowls' 'eads! Ye'll suffocate 'em!'

We would scatter corn far and wide, making sure that

Granny's special love, her Rhode Island Red, had her fair share. Sometimes Granny's chickens got in with ours, or ours got in with Granny's. Tiny would then herd them up and make sure that the right ones got sent back into the right runs. Sometimes we let them out just for the fun of seeing my lovely little dog separate them. She never made a mistake, that clever little dog. Granfer would tell us that we were 'bad little varmints', but we could tell that he enjoyed the show as much as we did. When he went to collect Billy Pony, he let us tag along and never minded how slow we were. We would get distracted on the way and stop here and there to pick a bunch of buttercups or daisies.

'Yer!' Granfer called, bending down. 'Do 'ee like butter?'

I would hold a buttercup under his chin.

'Yes, my pretty, I loves it – when I gits it!'

We laughed when he said this, because if anyone was likely to get butter, it was Mary Ann's Edwin. Granny made sure of that.

We would plod down the sunny lane, poking in the hedges for birds' nests, climbing on all the gates, sometimes having a swing on an open one, which we were not supposed to do.

'No, don't do that! Gates cost money and the hinges will break!'

We still did it if we thought we could get away with it.

'When I'm growed up, Rosie,' whispered Johnny, 'I'll 'ave a farm with lots o' gates and you an' me will swing on 'em all day long if we wants!'

Many years later, Johnny did buy a farm with lots of

gates, horses and other animals, but I think he was probably too busy to swing on those gates. When we got home, we gave our bunches of wild flowers to our mothers, and then watched Granfer brush Billy Pony's coat until it shone. He gave Billy a bucket of fresh water and a bag of oats, which he hung around his neck. Then Granfer sat in the sun in his old wooden armchair, and some of his younger grandchildren would sit on his lap while he held his pocket watch to their ears. We never guessed that each tick-tock was ticking our lives away, taking us all away from each other. But that was in the future. We lived in the here and now, and life was still a wonderful adventure.

My cousin Johnny died in his early sixties, but he had spent his whole life with animals, birds and all living things. He even got a horse and cart like Granfer's, in which he travelled all around the countryside, selling his fruit and vegetables, as fresh as a daisy, from house to house. He was a lovely boy. We did not see much of each other as adults, except at weddings and funerals, but I remember him with much affection, and still smile to think of me and Johnny, all growed-up and swinging on his gates.

My cousin Valerie said to me just the other day, 'We've had the best of both worlds, Rosie.' Yes, we have.

Epilogue

Endings

Granny lived to a good old age until she died one day of a stroke, when I was in my early twenties. I missed her more than I can say. We all did. Strangely, I thought Granny was invincible. I never imagined she could die, and life was never quite the same without her. Her funeral was just as lavish as Granfer's, and she was buried next to her Edwin. So Mary Ann and Edwin are together, as they were meant to be. The same cortège of Gypsy carts and horses followed Granny on her final journey, and the policemen directing the traffic may well have been the same ones as Edwin had years before. They too removed their helmets, saluted and bowed their heads.

'Well,' as Granny used to say, 'I wouldn't change places with the Queen!'

I truly believe that Granny deserved their respect. She had brought up her many children and worked hard all her life. She never missed a day taking out her heavy basket in all weathers (except when Granfer died), and she never claimed any benefits from the state but her few shillings of old-age pension.

Yes, Granny did it her way, and I believe that people like my granny and granfer make this world a better place; they made it so for us children, I do know that.

It has taken me a long time and a lot of thought to write about the death of my father, mainly because I never thought he would die. To me, he was invincible. He was never ill. I can never even remember him having the sniffles. As for lying around in bed – he was always up with the lark, having his morning wash and shave before he put the kettle on to make us all a cup of tea. He made so much noise, splashing the water everywhere, cleaning his lovely white teeth, gargling and then coughing when the water went down the wrong way. He had all his teeth except two, which he removed with his pliers. I actually saw him do it. I would have thought it would have been easier for him to go to the dentist, but Dad refused.

'No, I can bear me own pain, but not what's inflicted by someone else!' he explained, and so did it himself. He must have done something right, because his mouth healed perfectly. He was a great believer in the healing powers of salt water.

To me, Dad would always be there for us. Except one day, about ten years after Granny's death, Mum told us that my father was not feeling too good and the doctor had been called. He had told my mother that Dad had to rest.

'Rest?' Dad roared. 'Rest? How do 'ee think we can live if I rests?'

However, he had no choice in the matter because he had always been a strong man and now he was no longer. After a few days, he got up and went into the scrap yard, trying so hard to do a little bit. It was heartbreaking when he realised he could no longer earn his living, but he tried. Day after day he tried. Aunt Betsy set an old wooden armchair by the gate so that he could watch the comings and goings of everyone who visited the yard. He was not happy about this, but he had no choice. Sometimes he went out in the lorry with Alfie and Freddy just for the ride. I will always remember that, although Dad could no longer work, any money that was earned was still split three ways, and for years after Dad died, my mother still received his share of anything that was sold. Up until my mother received her pension, they would still give her unexpected sums of money. If my mother queried this, they would say that they had just sold something that had belonged to Dad. I knew this could not be true as the yard was regularly cleared, and so anything Dad had contributed to would have been sold years before. They did not have to do this, but it was certainly appreciated by my mother and all of us, especially as some weeks they just scraped by.

Dad had some X-rays done at the local hospital, which revealed several problems, chiefly heart trouble. As a young man he had contracted rheumatic fever and his heart was enlarged. He had been told in his early twenties that he would never walk without a stick, maybe two, and would end up in a wheelchair. Well, as a small child I do remember Dad having a walking stick. He used it for pulling down the brambles when we went blackberry picking. My mother told me that one day, a year or so after having to use the sticks, he threw them away from him in a rage and said, 'I'll never walk with sticks again!'

As far as I know, he never did. Even when he was becoming frail he did not use his sticks, and he still went down the pub for his pint. Even though I knew that Dad was very ill, I buried my head in the sand. If I did not think about it, it would not happen. Then one day, as I sat talking to my mother, he made a little joke and he laughed. I turned to speak to him and my heart seemed to stop for a few seconds as he stopped laughing and leaned back against his pillows. Death looked out of his face, and I knew he would not be with us for much longer. Sure enough, the doctor told my mother he would have to go into hospital the very next day. The same night, he fell out of his hospital bed and when I went to see him, I was shocked to see him with a cut head and a black eye. He looked dreadful. All the time my mother had looked after him he had never fallen. I felt very upset. Mum had been visiting him in hospital every day to make sure he was eating his meals, but his mind was wandering. He kept asking me if 'the boys', meaning Alfie and Freddy, were working in the yard as he could not hear them working.

Suddenly, buttoning up his pyjama jacket, he said, 'I'm just going out for a pint.' I tried to tell him he could not go out as he was in hospital.

'All right,' he said, 'will 'ee get me one?'

'I'll try,' I lied. I knew, at that time, that they would not allow it.

That night he died. I have always regretted that I did not at least try and get him his drink. When I told my mother how I felt, she just smiled.

'Think of the nice things you did for him. You must have made him dozens of sausage rolls!'

That made me laugh, as he loved my sausage rolls.

There were no young policemen standing with bowed heads as my father's cortège passed by. Times had changed. But the little church was packed full with many standing outside. I do not remember much of the service. It was a bitterly cold day in December. I could not stop shivering. I felt as though I would never be warm again.

My mother stood at the grave's edge. She looked so tiny, and very pale. I saw that my brother held her hand, and I was glad. I felt that at that moment, I could not comfort anyone else. I was trying to cope with my own feelings of loss. Dad was sixty-three, and that was many years ago now, but every time we have a new baby in the family I think, your granfer would have loved you. Our twins were just seven weeks old when Dad died, which was such a shame. He did see the babies several times beforehand, though, and I know he would have loved to have seen them growing up. The last time he saw them he gave me some money for them, which I quietly returned to Mum as I did not know if she had enough to manage on. That was just like him; generous as always. I made sure the twins knew who their granfer was, and showed them his photograph often.

Aunt Betsy lived until she was ninety-two, and died peacefully while sitting in her armchair. Most of her life she rarely sat down as she was always busy cooking, cleaning and looking after others. She was my father's sister, and they were close in age. Many were the magnificent rows they had. She used to hide her brooms because she said that my father was always losing them. My father spent ages hunting for them, wasting time he said, but they were soon friends again.

Much later, when Dad was ill and he sat by the gate in the old wooden armchair she set there for him, she kept him well provided with cups of tea and snacks. For years after he died she left the chair where she had set it for him, and often ran her hands over the back of it as she passed as though he was still there.

She tended the small patch of garden by the camp gate. Every year the daffodils she had planted came up.

'Our Eddy loved the daffs,' she commented. One year, for some reason, no flowers appeared. Nothing daunted, Betsy collected the free plastic daffodils from the packets of washing powder and stuck them into the small patch of earth. They looked very realistic – from a distance. They fooled quite a lot of people, who praised her unusual floral display. The one person who would never have been fooled was my father. He would have spotted a fake straight away, and in fact hated plastic flowers, but Aunt Betsy was happy and they brightened up an empty spot.

There was standing-room only in the church that day, when he was buried. In one of the many letters my mother received after his death, I read: 'He will always be missed, but most of all we will miss his wonderful laugh.'

Whenever I think of my father, I can see him standing with his thumbs tucked into his braces, his head thrown back, laughing and laughing. When he went into the village to get a few bits and pieces, he often gave a few coppers to any small children he saw gazing into the sweet-shop windows, if he had any to spare, that is. Can you imagine anyone doing that today? But that was my father's way. He loved to give.

Dad gave us another wonderful memory to keep. I remember being sworn to secrecy, and that we must never tell any of our schoolfriends what we were about to see. We solemnly swore we would tell no one, 'God's honour!' To us that was a sacred promise we would never break.

It was a perfect day, warm, sunny with a soft breeze. We quietly trooped along, a little band of Gypsy kids; we must have looked quaint. We went across the fields and along the riverbank as quiet as mice, just as we had been told. Then Dad stopped by a big old tree and told us to sit and not say a word or even laugh. We crouched silently for a very long time and then, suddenly there was a ripple in the water, a soft splash and three small furry bodies appeared on the riverbank. Otters! We all gasped softly. Oh, how beautiful they were as they frolicked and gambolled on the bank and in the river, two babies and their mother! We sat transfixed all morning, not wanting to leave, but in the end we had to, of course. We had no camera with us, but I did not need one because even now, more than sixty years later, the memory is still as fresh as it was the day we saw the otters.

I suppose by today's standards Dad wasn't a very good father, but all I know and remember is that I always felt happy in his company, and I always knew where to find him. He was proud of anything we accomplished and taught me much, maybe unknowingly, about our Creator, who I knew and loved long before I could read or write, and for this alone I am more than grateful to him.

Recently I bumped into Aunt Brit's girls, and I mentioned how much I loved their mother. They laughed and told me that Aunt Mary, as they called my mother, was so lovely to them that they had often wished she was *their* mother! We always feel the grass is greener on the other side of the fence.

As Mum grew older, I felt concerned that my life was so busy that I could not spend as much time with her as I wanted. So my brothers and my girls decided to find out if she would move nearer to us if she could. She said she would. So we managed to obtain a tenancy on a one-bedroom bungalow for her. It was very nice, with a small garden. We took her to see it, and left her alone to wander round to think about it. When she came out, she was smiling.

'Yes. It's lovely. And it's got a *garden*!' she said.

She spent six years in her little home, looking after her garden and making it comfortable. I went to see her one Friday in October. We had a cup of tea and we set the world to rights. As I was leaving, she put something into my hand.

'Here you are, Rosie,' she said. 'Buy yourself something nice.'

She was always doing this.

'No, Mum. You've only got a pittance. Buy yourself something!'

'I've got all I need,' she replied, shaking her head, and added, 'You've always been there for me, Rosie.'

Those were the last words she ever spoke to me. She did not turn up to meet me the following day, as usual. It had been my ritual for years to meet on a Saturday at two o'clock outside Marks and Spencer's in town, rain or shine, to do a bit of shopping with her. That Saturday I waited and waited, but she did not come. I knew in my heart something was not right. I got straight back on the bus home, my heart pounding all the way. As soon as I got in, I found my husband down his shed.

'John. Take me over Mum's. Something's wrong.'

He dropped everything and got the car out. When we pulled up outside the bungalow, I noticed a newspaper hanging out of the letterbox. I knew. I just *knew*. John got out and looked through the window. As I approached, he turned and put his arms around me.

'Oh, Rose. She's gone.'

She had just sat down and died. The doctor said it had been very quick. Her newspaper had slid down off her lap and her spectacles were still in her hand, as though she had just fallen asleep while reading the paper. Her neighbour told me that Mum had been in her garden the day before, cutting back her rose bushes. That was Mum. She lived until she died. But it was a terrible shock to me. Seventeen years have passed, and I miss her still. She was blessed to die so peacefully in her own home, with dozens of photographs of her family all around her, looking forward to a day out with me.

Rosina was in Germany when my mother died. She spoke to me on the telephone. The line crackled, and at first I could not recognise her voice as her German accent was so strong. You would have thought she was a German born and bred. She talked of Mum so lovingly, and remembered how kind Mum had always been to her, which was so very comforting. After our little chat I laughed to myself to think that Rosina had not changed a bit. She was still mimicking the people she was with. She was more German than the Germans!

Violet moved to Canada in later years, and we spoke on the telephone. She too is still the same, and made me laugh, which was good. We spoke of Mum, our childhood and all the happy memories we had as children in the little camp we called home, and the surrounding countryside which became our playground. All good memories.

My brothers found their places in life, too. In adulthood, their lives continued to be connected to the open air: Nelson worked on the farms nearby, Teddy worked for the Forestry Commission and Christopher took his place with my uncles and father in the family scrap business.

*

Granny always said that the land she bought belonged to all of her children, and that we could live on it as long as we wanted to. When no one wanted to live there any longer, then we could sell the land, but all the surviving children must agree on the sale. She did not leave a will but the land was lived on until well into this century until, in accordance with Granny's wishes, all agreed to the sale of the land.

In the thirties, when Granny bought her fields and a paddock, she paid one hundred and fifty pounds cash; she could not have visualised that it would ever be sold. I am happy, as most of us are, that it was bought by a young member of the family, who has put half down to grass and the other half, where my family lived, has not been touched. It remains the focal point of all our memories. I still live just eight miles away, and I often pop in to Carol and Henry's place, which is their childhood home, adjacent to Granny's old place. Dear Henry is nearly eighty years old now, and has the gentle nature he inherited from Uncle Fred. My cousin Carol, his sister, still looks after him with as great a care as she did her own parents.

Whenever I pass the old Gypsy encampment, I see Granny's hut is still there, falling to pieces now, as is the standpipe and tap that served us so well for many years. My mother's little strip of garden is overgrown, but the peach tree she grew still stands. The strawberry plants and raspberry canes, which bore wonderful soft fruit for us, now entangled with wild flowers, stretch towards the old apple tree that still bears pink blossoms in the spring and in summer. The lily of the valley my mother loved so much still scents the air as it mingles with my memories of night-scented stocks and mignonette on warm summer nights. If I close my eyes, I can almost hear the voices of the boys who lived down the road and the melancholy sound of the harmonica they played, harmonising their voices as they drifted home from a night out. When I think of the lives that were lived there in that small community, almost like a small village, I think the air must still echo with our laughter and childish voices calling to each other.

'It's time for school, Baby Bet! Come on, it's ten to eight!'

'Come and play, Vi!'

'Let's go blackberry picking, Rosie!'

'Granny! Granfer! Come and see!'

For those who shared the life and the love, the joys and the sorrows of daily life on Granny's land, the memories will never fade or die, and the singing and laughter will resonate on the breeze for ever more.

Yes, the road we travel from childhood to old age is long and so full of special moments that trying not to return is an impossible task, and I do it often in my memory. The comfort and pleasure it has brought me is beyond compare, a wonderful gift and a joy to share. So beautiful and perfect those moments are, and yet as fleeting as a field full of butterflies on a warm summer day, free to fly, and yet captured for ever in memories.

Romany Words

I cannot say that we were in any sense of the word bilingual, but we mixed up Romany words with English words in such a way that it was difficult for a listener to understand what we were saying. For instance, 'Pouve da gry' means 'Put the horse in the field', and 'Dikai at rahni' means 'Look at the lady'. My spelling of the Romany words may not be correct, as I have never seen these words written down by a Gypsy. They have been passed down by word of mouth. I heard my granny and granfer use them sometimes, but because my mother was *gadje* I heard a watered-down version as it was mixed with English. We could talk among ourselves if we were in the company of *gadjes* and did not want to be understood. I have heard Londoners use the word 'chavvy' for child, which is Romany, also 'kushti' for 'good' and 'vonger' for money. Here are some more I remember:

Dikai – look out
Av – come
Rhy – gentleman
Rakli – woman

Tan – tent
Rhyni – posh woman
Jukel – dog
Dinlo – stupid person
Drom – road
Didacoi – pretend Romany
Vardoe – caravan, cart or wagon
Dukker – haggle or beg

I have heard some Indian words that I recognise, which sound similar to Romany, that I have heard spoken by the travelling Gypsies I met. This is not surprising as Romanies are said to have their roots in India and then travelled across Europe with their traditions and skills, living a nomadic life mainly because they were not welcome in many places. Gypsies have been in England for more than seven centuries, and will hopefully be here for many centuries to come.